Charles H Reeve

The Prison Question

Charles H Reeve

The Prison Question

ISBN/EAN: 9783743392694

Manufactured in Europe, USA, Canada, Australia, Japa

Cover: Foto ©ninafisch / pixelio.de

Manufactured and distributed by brebook publishing software (www.brebook.com)

Charles H Reeve

The Prison Question

THE PRISON QUESTION.

A THEORETICAL AND PHILOSOPHICAL REVIEW OF SOME
MATTERS RELATING TO CRIME, PUNISHMENT, PRIS-
ONS, AND REFORMATION OF CONVICTS. WITH A
GLANCE AT MENTAL, SOCIAL AND POLITICAL
CONDITIONS; AND SOME SUGGESTIONS
ABOUT CAUSES, AND THE PRE-
VENTION OF CRIME AND
THE PRODUCTION OF
CRIMINALS.

DESIGNED TO SHOW HOW SOCIETY MAY PROTECT ITSELF AGAINST THE
DISORDERLY ELEMENTS, AND CHECK THE RAPID IN-
CREASE OF THE PRISON POPULATION.

*All of our efforts will fail unless we adapt our methods to the
operation of the natural forces.*

BY

CHARLES H. REEVE.

CHICAGO:
KNIGHT & LEONARD CO., PRINTERS,
1890.

.

PRESS OF
KNIGHT & LEONARD CO.,
CHICAGO.

CONTENTS.

4 CONTENTS.

CHAPTER XI.

CHAPTER XII.

CHAPTER XIII.

CHAPTER XIV.

CHAPTER XV.

INTRODUCTORY.

S OME noted man—perhaps the Rev. Sidney Smith—was asked to review a book, and this was his review: "Most of it is old. What is old has been better said before. What is new had better not been said." Some who read this little book may be disposed to take such a view of it; but new or old, well or ill said, the truths stated in it cannot be found elsewhere associated together in application to the prison question, nor addressed to the common comprehension which it is desirable to reach. Discussions on the subject here treated, have been mostly before learned bodies and in scientific language. The common readers, to whom this is addressed, have given but little attention to the subject-matter, and it is important that they should give more. Reformers and prison officials may find things in it they can use to advantage. It is not expected that its contents will meet with general approval and acceptance, nor that it will escape criticism and perhaps some ridicule. It would be commonplace if it should. It contains statements of fact, which, if seriously considered in the connection they are here placed and sought to be applied, must be of value; and when so considered they will be likely to modify some prevailing opinions, to the betterment of the unbalanced classes as well as of the general community, whatever may provoke that consideration.

The fundamental propositions laid down in this book were outlined by me in a public lecture twelve years ago, and were urged with some emphasis. They were briefly urged in

papers read by me before the National Prison Congress at
Detroit in October, 1885, on "The True Theory of Reform,"
at Boston in July, 1888, on "Dependent Children" and at
Nashville in November, 1889, on "Arousing the Public." My
aim in this little book has been, to group some important,
well-established facts and apply them to the subjects of
prisons and reforms, in such order as will interest the general
public so far as I can reach it ; and so aid in creating a public
opinion that can intelligently and practically deal with and
dispose of the defective classes and the causes that produce
them.

THE PRISON QUESTION.

CHAPTER I.

THE PRISON QUESTION.

IN 1878, I read a paper before the Philosophical Society of Chicago on the "Rationale of Punishment" for public offences. The views then briefly presented are elaborated in this work. They were in advance of the times then, but experience and concurrence of thought have shown them to be generally correct, and they are being tried in practice in some respects to a limited extent, in some localities. The time is not distant when the public opinion will fully endorse them, and become more radical in its efforts to suppress vice than is herein suggested. The ideas advanced have passed beyond the mere force of propositions, and sooner or later, to careful observers, they will be regarded as real theories, because they are in harmony with their environment, and will continue to be so as the field of inquiry and development grows larger.

The rapid and alarming increase in the numbers of criminals and in the extension of the planes on which they act, as well as of increase of the demented, and the professional paupers,— being out of proportion to increase of population,—present problems for solution in social, political and mental science, that call for the continued and diligent efforts of the ablest minds in the land. An impractical theology on one hand, and a blind agnosticism on the other, when applied to the subject, the one misdirecting practical energy and true humanity by a dogmatic view of Special Providence, and the other breeding a disposition to construe liberty to mean license, and hence, a misappropriation and misuse of privileges, have brought about and are maintaining conditions that operate to prevent a true solution of these problems; while they also beget and force into practice, propositions and efforts in the name of reforms, that are false in conception and failures in practice.

That from a false position no step can be taken in advance without plunging into more falsities, is a fact so self-evident that it precludes argument. The only practical steps are such as lead to a true position. That attained, practical forward movement can be made; keeping a wary eye for tempting but impractical by-ways, and moving no faster than demonstration shows to be warranted. There can be no solution of problems in mathematics unless the local and relative value of figures and symbols be maintained. So in other cases. The conditions and operative forces must be studied, and all efforts must be adapted to them if they are to be made practical. In the discussions that have attended the efforts of reformers, and that have finally grown into what is called the prison question, many elements and opinions exist that should be eliminated at this time, and others be brought forward, in order to an understanding of what that question presents. In order to answer it correctly the whole subject-matter should be relieved of many garments that have been put upon it, giving it a false appearance.

The question is much like an issue made up in court to be tried. As the allegations are, so must the evidence be; and parties and advocates must confine themselves to the record, for justice is inflexible. The issue is the skeleton. The proofs are the garments to clothe it, and the court and jury, directed by the law, are to see that they are put on in the right way and place, and send it forth as the work of justice; an evidence of the power of the law through the court to enforce what is right and prohibit what is wrong. Sentimentalisms are wholly out of place in it. Mercy comes after justice. "Mercy seasons justice." There can be no mercy until there is first justice. Justice is born of necessity and must be measured by it. In the prison question the criminal and his mentality is the issue, the environments—the social, political, and statutory conditions—are the evidence, and the natural forces operate as the law. Justice regards not simply the welfare of the criminal, but of the public and of individuals as well, in all relations.

If we take the position of the theologian, that a Special Providence is necessary and it must be invoked or all efforts will fail, we must bear in mind that the great law of equilibration is coeval with that Providence and is a part of it; and that Providence itself will not interfere with its operations, lest it destroy the equilibrium of the universe. It is operative in every atom, and in every force inherent in matter. Whatever Providence does He will do through the natural and material agencies of the plane on which action is taken. When the bully went to a clergyman's house to whip him for interfering on behalf of one of his parishioners and breaking up a proposed marriage, he said to the clergyman, "I suppose you expect Providence to protect you?" "Yes," said the clergyman, quickly pushing up his sleeves and letting his fist go, "and this is the instrument he will use;" and he knocked the ruffian clear down the steps onto the sidewalk, putting him *hors du combat.* We must adopt that theologian's view. "Providence helps those who help themselves;" that is, by natural laws He has placed within our reach every needed element and tells us to help ourselves. In this way and this only will there be any interference in our behalf—by adapting ourselves to our environments, and making the best use we can of the opportunities within our reach.

If we take the view of the materialist—that there is no Providence, and that annihilation follows the end of conscious existence—we must bear in mind that the universal desire to escape that annihilation has created and maintains a widespread belief in a Providence; and whatever creates and sustains a hope of a higher and better life hereafter, carries with it a fear of not attaining it; and that hope and fear combined, will hold millions who so believe to a moral life, who would be lawless without it. Both the theologian and materialist should recognize the fact that, to work together for a common end in efforts to solve what is called the prison question, they must get onto the mental and moral level of the crime class in order to comprehend the people there, and be comprehended by them; for unless there is mutual comprehension the higher cannot raise the lower, and there can be no permanent reform of prisons, prisoners, or those from among whom prisoners come. If there is mutual comprehension of the theological plane, and mutual belief in any case, and reform so comes, well and good; that case was a right use of opportunities. But if there be no such comprehension the theologian will fail as a reformer in every such case. If on the other hand, there be a mutual comprehension on the plane of the materialist, and the moral perception is so enlarged that observance of order and justice follows, the materialist will succeed; otherwise, he will fail as a reformer. If both fail, then physical force alone remains for both.

But there is a plane for action common to both, and united effort on that plane will accomplish all that is possible to be done, and the object of this work is, to so deal with the facts as to disclose it and so make the way clear to an answer to the prison question. It would be futile to preach Christianity to a Jew or a Mohammedan. His moral perceptions, or fears, or hopes must be reached through channels where he can see the way. It would be a waste of labor to try to beat the Christian theology into the mind of an ignorant, brutal boor, full of superstitions. In a word, reformers must bridge the chasm · between orthodoxy and heterodoxy, spiritualism and materialism, and cross and re-cross as may be necessary to get to the level of the individual who is to be taught to recognize and live in a moral atmosphere. With convicts, the aim is, to induce them to observe civil order. Any influence which will accomplish that, should be used.

Up to this time the knowledge and opinions on the subject have been more of accidental growth than the result of specific designs and practical efforts from philosophical deductions. During the time when convicts were denied all means for protection when under charge and on trial, and all means for relief under conviction, when they were regarded as outlaws and subjected to severe penalties, with fixed terms, denied every comfort, herded together without distinction as to previous or present conditions, and generally treated worse than brutes, philanthropy, based on emotional pity, sought entrance to the prisons in two forms: one, that of John Howard, to amel-

iorate the prisoner's hard lot ; the other, that of church consola-
tion.   The prison authorities generally regarded both with dis-
favor; but the knowledge of facts about prisons thus gained,
was carried out, and in time came before the public.   An opinion grew that forced improvements.   Charitable societies
formed and aid was given to discharged prisoners, and discipline became more humane.   Legislation was invoked and
criminal laws were modified.   Mentality, society and politics
were classed among subjects for scientific investigation and
study, but while what now is called the prison question involved them all more than did any other subject, it was not
so regarded in the general perception, or even in that of a
majority of the reformers.

As always happens with social and political innovations,
reformers dealt with results rather than with causes, while in
fact, the answer to the prison question must be found in the
causes of the conditions rather than in the conditions; to
which, thus far inquiry has been largely confined.   Gradually,
a consciousness of this fact dawned upon a few here and there,
but it was running counter to the main currents of opinion to
attempt to direct attention to the real causes, and few had
the courage to attempt it with a hope that attention could be
secured.   The inquiry into the conditions of prisons and of
convicts in them, how to make them more comfortable, and
give the convicts better surroundings than many honest laboring people outside had who were taxed to support them, was
exhaustive ; and great improvements resulted for the convict.
But the real origin of the conditions and operative forces that
produced the fast increasing numbers of criminals and convicts, received comparatively little attention.

It must now be conceded that a demand for inquiry into the
causes, and means for their removal, enters more largely into
the prison question than does any other; and until that inquiry receives the attention a true reform demands and makes
necessary, the prison question will not be solved nor will any
actual advance be made of permanent character in reform ;
that is, a reform that aids in removing the cause while amelior-
ating the resulting conditions.   There can be no permanent
reform of any evil while the cause of the evil sought to be

reformed remains in operative force. If I shall succeed in directing the attention of even a few to the causes that produce and maintain the crime class and that stand in the way of reform, my labor will not have been in vain.

When Jesus Christ began in Judea to preach a radical revolution, one that was at war with the beliefs, prejudices and passions that had been the growth of centuries, he created antagonisms which gave existence to energies that created a religious belief for one-third—and the most intellectual—of the human race, besides causing his own crucifixion. It is so in part with every one who advocates anything that runs counter to the current public opinion; they create antagonisms. The seeds of truth thus sown will germinate sooner or later; and the generation that recognizes their existence and value will cultivate them. When recognized, there will be a truer and a higher civilization. Error is the mother of mysticism and superstition, and these are the parents of science. Nothing can exist without an opposite. Everything exists in its opposite. There can be no light without darkness, no hope without despair, no truth without error, no ignorance without knowledge, no love without hate, no death without life, no crime without order, no good without evil, and so on of everything in existence. Even the Bible could not create a God to worship without a Devil to antagonize Him, nor a heaven for the righteous without a hell for the wicked.

Everything that comes into existence brings in equilibrium the elements of good and evil, either in itself or in its relation to other things. To derive the most from the good and confine the evil in such channels as will effect the least injury is all that can be attained; and to this end the intelligence of men should be directed and their energies be exerted.

The correlation and conservation of forces is eternal, and the law of equilibration will be eternally operative. It applies to the conditions of men individually and socially in all relations, as it does to matter in all forms and conditions; and no theory of reform can be made operative for good that does not recognize these facts, and endeavor to shape all efforts in conformity to them. Let us see if an examination of a few fundamental truths, and of some conditions as they exist, will enable us to more clearly comprehend this so-called " Prison Question."

A full consideration of the subject involves directly and collaterally, not simply the convicts, but all of the defective classes.· The incurably diseased, the insane, the weak-minded and idiotic, all who are mentally defective and unbalanced, the vicious, the criminally inclined, and the hereditary pauper and vagabond classes from which they largely come. It demands consideration of the relations that exist between society and government on the one hand and these classes on the other; and the real question is, what duty does the sound, moral, orderly and self-supporting portion of the population *owe to themselves* in view of these classes? They alone can organize and maintain government and constitute orderly society; and they alone must carry the burdens. The duty they *owe to these classes*—which has been largely considered to this time—will be disclosed in fully considering this question.

CHAPTER II.

THE first thing that confronts us when we come to the consideration of the criminal class, is the mentality of the individual. That mentality is dependent on the quality of brain and nerve substance, the volume and arrangement of brain ganglia, and the impressions made on body and brain by environment. Science has demonstrated that each particular function of what we call mind has its special location and is centered in some local part of the brain-substance called a ganglion; which can be removed and that part of the mind will be gone and the function located there be lost. Using the description of another for brevity, I will try to make the idea clear to the common mind.

The brain contains two kinds of matter, one white and the other gray. The medulla oblongata at the base of the brain connects it with the spinal cord. From the spinal cord nerves extend through the bony spinal column in two sets, consisting of gray matter and white. One matter conveys the energy that gives the sense of feeling and the other the energy that gives the power of motion. Others from the medulla and lower brain supply the face, throat, etc. With each thought and each motion a portion of the tissue is consumed and the waste must be supplied by proper nutriment, digested, and carried by the blood, and taken up by the formative vessels adapted to that work.

"Experiments in vivisection (dissection and examination of living animals) demonstrated that the whole brain above the medulla could be removed and the animal functions of the body would go on. The higher brain could be removed and as long as the medulla was uninjured the remaining brain would perform its functions. For instance, the higher parts of the brain were removed from a pigeon, and it showed indifference when let alone, but under the stimulus of electricity it would live. If laid on its back it would regain its feet. If pinched it would walk away. If thrown in the air it would use its wings and descend in its usual manner. Light would make the the pupils òf the eyes contract. If ammonia was held to its nose it would draw back in disgust. It made no effort to feed itself, but would swallow food when put in its mouth, and would die of starvation if not artificially fed. So in frogs and fishes. With the higher portions of the brain removed, a fish will go on swimming until its course is impeded. It will take no food and will die of starvation. A frog will move about in the water until it reaches land and then will sit indifferent. If stroked on the back it will croak.

"So in man, certain subdivisions of his faculties correspond to certain subdivisions of the brain. The medulla, as stated, is the connecting link between the spinal cord and the brain, and its most important function is to regulate the respiratory movements. The paralysis of some nerve centers or blood vessels in the medulla is called sun-stroke or heat-stroke and causes death. The medulla controls the movements of swallowing; it contains the center for the physiognomical play of the muscles of the face and another for articulated words. All of its functions are mechanical or automatic, and will continue when the higher brain has been removed or is impaired by disease.

"The affections, fear, terror, pleasure, pain, etc., are functionated in the second division of the brain,—the optic lobes or bridge.

"The cerebellum or little brain is the third division. It is the organ of equilibration. The animal from which it has been removed staggers and appears drunk. One part of the cerebellum prevents man from falling forward, another from falling backward, another from turning around in a circle.

"The central ganglia are the fourth division and they enable us to do many complex things in a mechanical way; to walk while thinking or reading; to play music while thinking of something entirely different; to sew, knit and talk without paying much attention to it.

"The highest division of the brain, its gray matter, is the fifth division. This is the portion that may be called the seat of the soul. It is not a single organ, but consists of a number of differentiated organs, each one of which is possessed of certain functions, yet is in the closest possible connection with all the others.

"To define all these various organs with accuracy, to define their intimate structure as well as their individual energy, and to trace the physiological and pathological alterations which they undergo during the natural process of development, maturity and decay, and in diseases to which they are subject, is the greatest problem for the anatomy and physiology of the twentieth century; and when it is solved a complete revolution in psychology must result."

With these facts before us, what a view is presented in this prison question! What possible solution can there be of any value unless these facts are carefully considered in studying the criminal class and the causes of crime? In that study we are met at the threshold by two things that claim our attention. The first is, the fact that no impression can be made upon the brain ganglions but such as come through the channels of the senses, and the other is, the origin and character of the material that make up the body and brain of the individual. If the origin is vicious and the material coarse the impressions made and retained will be different under the same environment from what they would be with the origin moral and the material fine. So if the origin be fine and the material good, but the environment be coarse or vicious, the impressions made and remaining will be different from either of the others.

Again, the physical development of the body will greatly modify the character of impressions. If digestion and powers of assimilation be good and the environment be coarse the fibre produced to supply waste will not be such as it would be with better fare, nor the impressions be the same. If the physical powers be weak, digestion and assimilation imperfect, the physical and mental results will be materially modified. There is a conscious intelligence in matter which, when left to itself and unobstructed in its processes, makes no mistakes. For instance, take a preparation of corn meal in the form of food and feed it to a sheep and it will make mutton, tallow and wool. If given to a hog it will make pork, lard, hair and bristles. If given to a negro it will make black skin, kinky hair, flat nose, thick lips, and an imitative, non-progressive brain energy. If given to a white man it will make a white skin, various colored straight hair, various colored eyes, shapely limbs and features, a higher quality of brain and an original, progressive brain energy. In each of these the brain fibre will be different and the impressions through the senses unlike. In each there will be higher and lower types of both physical and mental construction, and outgrowth consequent. With iron, brass and silver we make progressively, finer castings and polish, and they are progressively subject to oxydation in the same order, the coarsest more, the finer less. So with the body; the coarser the fibre the less susceptible of fine impressions, the less capable of comprehending and acting under moral perception. The finer the fibre the more susceptible to higher impressions. Then comes the arrangement of ganglions and the impressions made, whether coarse or fine, to determine the controlling energy under which the individual will act. In dealing with criminals with a view to reformation we must become advised of the physical construction of the individual, quality of material, existence of brain ganglia, their combinations, and the impressions already made. If what is lacking to a true moral perception can be supplied and what is obstructed can be removed, reformation is possible; but it is not, otherwise. The character, quality and arrangement of brain ganglia with the impressions made upon them constitute the elements of mentality and source of mental energy of the individual.

CHAPTER III.

A SCIENTIST or philosopher must have opinions and form theories, but he recognizes that a proposition is a theory only when it agrees with its environments; and he bends his energies to ascertain the exact truth regardless of the fate of his opinions. If the truth makes for or against his opinions his search is directed to the discovery and elucidation of facts as they exist and their bearing on other facts already known; his opinions or theories being among the elements directing his efforts. He is no scientist who searches alone for facts to sustain a theory and rejects all that are opposed to his theory.

In using the word "education" in connection with this branch of my subject, I mean to include the knowledge acquired from all sources; the surroundings and associations of the individual as well as that from teaching and books. In using the words "mental organization," or "organism," I mean to include the brain and the whole nerve structure, its sources of supply, growth, progress, waste, deterioration, and the causes; the quantity and quality of brain and nerve matter and the influence that affect each and all in a material way, internal, external, directly and relatively. Mind and its operations, in directing the acts of the rest of the body, depend on all and not on a part, and the act is a result of all and not of a part. Human beings are as unlike in these things as they are in their looks, manners and acts.

The word "mentality" will express the energy that is produced by the mental organization, the capacity to receive impressions, and manifest the impulses they prompt. The word "mentalism" will include the perceptions, the impulses, the opinions, the beliefs, and general "isms" that are the actual outgrowths of that mentality. I use this order regardless of lexicons and ordinary definitions.

It cannot be denied that great intellect and great passions and appetites go together, in some form, and it is always a question which will dominate.   It depends largely on environment and education.   I do not use the word passion in the sense usually understood only.   Its manifestations are endless.   It may be in the direction of wine, women, sporting, penuriousness, senseless extravagance, inordinate ambition, brainless adventure, love of tyranny, love of notoriety, and other outlets.   The intellect may vitiate the passions and appetites, or they may be vicious by inheritance and the intellect may increase or diminish the vicious quality.   We may compare the mental organization to a motive power and working machinery.

The vital source of energy in the human structure—whatever and wherever it may be—commonly supposed to center in the base of the brain, may be called the engine, supplied by the functions of the body as a boiler, and in turn enabling the body to supply itself, aided by reciprocal energy.   The intellect or higher brain may be called the working machinery. If the machinery is large and either rapid moving and incisive, or ponderous and slow-moving but powerful, the motive power must be capable of moving it properly and be adapted to it. The so-called moral sentiments may be called the regulating machinery; the feed, exhaust, governors, cut-offs, cams, levers, guides, friction rollers, and other adjustments controlling the motive power on one hand and the movements of the working machinery on the other.

First, that capacity of the regulating machinery to admit of adaptation, and second, the method of adaptation, determines whether the power shall control the working machinery for good or for evil.   For want of proper control shall the intellect be used, finally, to feed the motive power—the appetites and passions—or shall the motive power be controlled and used to exert the intellect for great and useful ends?   The brightest intellects never reach full maturity.   Dazzled by their own light, no adjustment controls them and they dash wildly to their own destruction.   The world is full of instances.

The small but incisive intellect may have great animal

brain behind it and the moral brain be wholly overborne. The great intellect may have small animal and small moral powers and be weakly vicious. The great and active intellect and great animal brain may go together and have no sufficient moral governor, and become great in vice. It may have moral balance but be improperly educated; or be surrounded by evil influences if rightly educated, and so the intellect be dominated by the animal. We may have a fair balance of brain organization educated, and yet, from some idiosyncrasy have a lack of moral perception. Of this we have a striking illustration in the South. Where there used to be an hundred negro convicts in the penitentiary there are now six hundred, and the increase comes mostly from among the educated negroes. The increased intelligence is used to secure the gratification of the impulses of the animal rather than for the elevation of the intellectual man.

In all cases it depends materially on circumstances which will dominate and in many cases the actual character of brain tissue, the sources of supply and process of waste, must be considered as circumstances. We may take illustrations of the principle from among noted men. Eugene Aram, Dr. Webster, of Boston, and Monroe Edwards as exhibiting one phase ending in the highest grade of crimes. As an example in two directions we may take Daniel Webster. As examples of vicious ambition, selfishness, jealousy, and criminal revenge, we may take Aaron Burr and Benedict Arnold. For thieves, embezzlers and swindlers, with fine ability, classical education, and years in positions of trust, we can take our penitentiaries, and the cities of Canada with their refugees. The illustrations cited are merely to emphasize the proposition that strong intellect and strong animal impulses go together, and it depends largely on accidental circumstances which will dominate.

Strong physical energy manifests itself in bodily activity when of a kind to feed and sustain active mental energy. When not of that kind it may be perfect in its automatic action of supply and waste of tissue, and averse to bodily activity. Strong mental energy when from organic combinations of ganglia that give versatility, stimulates bodily activity, whether the physical organism of the body be strong or weak. If weak, the mental energy soon consumes it. If in a strong body they will mutually stimulate activity. We have instances of weak and inferior development, both physical and mental, from sources where—from the parentage—we would expect the reverse. It can be accounted for only on the supposition of partial arrest of development during the period of utero-gestation, or some abnormal conditions following birth. On the other hand we find instances of strong bodily and mental development from sources where—from the parentage —it was not to be expected. In such case we look to like conditions in the remote ancestors, cropping out, or to unusual conditions occurring in the early life of the individual favorable to such development.

Let us consider the matter from a pathological point of view. A physician is called to attend on a sick man. He is compelled to take him just as he finds him and to diagnose his case from such facts as are within his reach. He does so, decides on the treatment, and makes a prognosis from the best light he has. At the next visit he may find that his diagnosis was not exactly right, or that the result of his treatment is not exactly what he hoped for, and, of course, his prognosis is wrong more or less. He diagnoses again from the changed conditions, varies the treatment and makes a new prognosis. He must depend on it until he has demonstration. And in this way he must go on from day to day. When he finds himself right, following out the indicated treatment, and when wrong, changing it. Convalescence and complete restoration may follow. Complications may intervene and still there may be recovery. Accidents may occur from neglect of a nurse, or from some death or calamity in the family; or from fire or other cause compelling hasty removal and exposure, or idiosyncrasies of constitution unknown to him may be inimical to certain remedies used; and the patient may linger, and arise thoroughly broken, or he may die. All may be right on the doctor's part and defects and impurities in the drugs used, unknown to him, may cause unfavorable results or failure, and he be never the wiser. But one fact is patent in case of failure, the patient is lost.

If the doctor be skilful he moves cautiously. He knows that nearly everything is hidden from him except the prominent symptoms. He palliates here, relieves there, stimulates one thing, narcotizes another, experiments where he must, and resorts to heroic treatment when emergencies demand it. But he watches results, waits when he can, studies effects and conditions, and constantly tries to see the way to relief and restoration.

Now let us take a child born into the world. No matter whether it be the offspring of prince or peasant, millionaire or pauper, scholar or ignorant boor, of hospital inmate or prison convict; we must take it as we find it. The physical organism, the character and arrangement of brain ganglia, the texture of fibre and tissue, the complete or partial development throughout, is all just what it is, and it is a living human being that may survive and become a factor in society and government. I repeat, we must take it with its environment just as they are, and the person who has the custody, and nurture and care of it occupies the exact position as to responsibility and duty which that physician did beside the bed of that sick patient, except that they are to treat both body and mind. Here is this visible beginning of physical and mental energy. From both may grow other forces capable of important results. Here is a body with the natural senses, and here is a brain to be fed in part by that body, using some of the senses, and to be impressed in other parts and become the seat of knowledge, developing mental energy, begetting impulses to be manifested in words and acts, making more or less impress on others with whom it will come in contact, and for good or evil. It is utterly helpless and can do nothing for itself in development of body or mind. First, it is wholly dependent on existing bodily conditions, and next, on environment now and henceforward. What will be the bodily and mental development? That will depend on the skill, treatment and attention of those rearing it. There will never come a time in its whole life when it will not be dominated by such energy as will be developed from the impressions made upon it continuously until it reaches what is called "the age of discretion," and that discretion will depend much on such impressions.

If the persons who nurture and rear this child are like the skilful doctor, they will pursue such a course as he did. They will study the child day by day, diagnose, decide on the management of it, and try to study results in advance from day to day, both as to physical and mental development, results of management and training, and watch and wait; changing diagnosis and treatment as developments indicate as far as knowledge will guide. It requires a sound body to develop and maintain a sound mind. Attention must be directed then to healthy bodily development, building up and strengthening what is weak or backward and suppressing what is over-developed and abnormal. As intelligence begins to dawn with perception and knowledge coming through the senses, the serious responsibility begins of studying the mental organization. As mentalisms develop themselves they are the visible symptoms; guided by them, it is possible to build up a strong and balanced mentality. If perceptions develop early and rapidly, and the child begins soon to notice and learns quick, shows signs of precocity, note the directions in which perception prompts impulses. For instance, if they tend to combativeness, destructiveness, and violent temper, try to divert attention, and guide impulses in some other direction until its attention can be gained, and begin to cultivate the perceptions and impulses that tend to balance these, and watch for exhibitions day by day. Try experiments and various plans to gain its attention in such directions as need cultivation, and away from such as are undesirable or over-developed.

If it develops slowly and seems to be stupid, try to stimulate perception in various ways, and note progress. In a word, encourage what seems latent and discourage what seems too forward. Endeavor to secure a balance as far as possible. Avoid antagonism whenever possible. The creation of a brutal fear will tend to rouse brutal antagonism—secrecy, caution, revenge, etc.; but at no time allow it to win in a controversy as to government. If diversion cannot be obtained after it is old enough to know, and restraint becomes necessary, make it effectual with as little pain as possible, and continue it until there is compliance; attended, however, with never varying kindness. Never tire of watching, and never urge or push until fatigue occurs in efforts to increase perception and knowledge. Convey lessons in play and amusements as soon and as fast as comprehension permits. Watch and care for physical development in the same way. In some cases the mother's milk may disagree and fail in digestion or assimilation. In such a case procure other source of sustenance. Some children will bear solid food much younger than others. Some organisms are subject to electric and magnetic influences with change of barmometer and thermometer, affecting both physicical and mental organization and changing the character and development in each. Some have a natural appetite for some special diet, such as meat, or acids, or sweets, and reject everything else. Some will assimilate what they crave and others will not, but will assimilate what they reject as distasteful. Some are easily chilled, others are full of sweat glands that are always active. Some will bear water and bathing, others will not; and in a family of children from one parentage there will be wide differentiation. One may have superior intellectual development and inferior animal or moral development, or there may be precocity in one direction, as to mathematics, drawing, or music. One may be garrulous, with or without easy flow of language, and another taciturn. One may be volatile, another steady. One may be mean and vicious in every way, another kind and amiable. In such cases the parents are unlike in most things, but the differences in the offspring is from natural mental organization, constantly increased by the supply of brain and nerve tissue, as well as from the arrangement and development of brain ganglia.

With proper training, each organism can be improved and brought more or less into proper balance. If left to itself or improperly trained, it is plain that the physical and mental energy will be just such as the organism will generate; and the mentalisms—the outgrowths and impulses—will be such as that energy produces. Nature is alike everywhere. A man bought a farm having an orchard. Originally, nice trees of the best grafted fruit had been set out, and they had been left to take care of themselves. No attention had been paid to soil, feeding, or trimming of roots or limbs. When in the way, large and small limbs had been clipped and without regard to the season when done; owing to this, on some, water sprouts were thick, on others rot had set in. Wind had leaned some of them over. Matured as it was, the new owner took it in hand. Where trees leaned, he trimmed the limbs so as to bring the top straight over the roots when it should be grown out. With others he removed roots on the side that grew too fast. He removed the scabby bark and washed with alkali. He gave the soil a proper dressing, removed water sprouts and painted the surface where all large branches were removed. He trimmed the tops out thin in February, and the wood hardened before the sap rose, drying up instead of rotting. In a few years he had a sightly orchard bearing fruit ; and although far from being what it might have been made with attention by the former owner from the time of planting, it was a great improvement on the dilapidated wreck he began on. Some trees were past all recovery and these were cut into wood.

His case was like that of a prison warden or governor of a reformatory, except that the latter's stock is not always from good origin. The physical and mental energy he found, (I use the words advisedly—contending for conscious intelligence in matter), he put in the best shape he could by looking at the case from a pathological point of view, giving such treatment as the case permitted and watching results.

I asserted that there is conscious intelligence in matter, and by proper use of our own intelligence we can furnish some elements where needed which matter will intelligently use to its own and our benefit. If a soil has become sour an alkaline dressing will be properly used by it in producing vegetation. Now this child we have called attention to comes forward to manhood and becomes a factor for good or ill, depending on all these chances I have specified or alluded to. If fortunate in birth and nurture it will be likely to be useful, developing healthy bodily and mental energy. If unfortunate in either, it may become the source of physical or mental evil, or of both. There is drifting in among the body of the people a continual flood of human organisms, the results of no design or calculation, or of preparation or care for them before or after birth, from every plane on which humanity moves or is found; and the great mass are the result of mere animal indulgence. When born, with the kindly and loving parents they are treated as pets and dolls. The idea of organization, of physical and mental formation and energy, is unthought of except in case of visible malformation, and then only in a purely mechanical sense. Ambition to have them appear smart, with some induces a senseless forcing process, and when grown the putting of them into a line of business for which they are in no way adapted. Such an idea as the study of mental pathology is never conceived, much less born and cultivated. Where the parents are unloving or brutal, a mere animal life is lived and energy of both body and brain finds its source in the impulses and acts generated from such conditions.

In proportion to the numbers in each, as many and perhaps more ill-balanced mentalities come from among the well-to-do classes than from those on a lower plane financially. Want of harmony in everything between the progenitors, and want of proper nurture and guidance during early development and during adolescent growth, produce the orchard referred to; and the prison wardens, under the most impractical legal provisions, and supervision of inexperienced directors, are charged with the duties of humane restraint and expected to work reformations, beginning with the gnarled, knotty, misshapen and ill-grown creatures where parents and guardians should have begun before and after birth; prepare for them, and when born, nurture, train, guide, and restrain them properly.

The law and its administrators could spend brains, time and money to advantage in providing for restraints, prohibitions and qualifications relating to those who would become parents, with better results and more public benefits than in permitting unbridled license, and then providing restraints, prohibitions and conditions for the ill-starred offspring of that license after they have become physical and mental crystallizations destructive of the public order.

To the development of healthy physical and mental energy, harmony in the progenitors of all the forces necessary, is a pre-requisite. We cannot "gather grapes from thorns, nor figs from thistles." Neither union or harmony can be secured by forcing a contact between inharmonious elements.

CHAPTER IV.

THEOLOGY.

IN the name of Christian theology the great body of reformers claim that there can be no reform of criminals without
a belief in the divinity of Christ, and through faith in the
saving influences of His crucifixion.

Theology—a science of God—is and must be based on
hypothesis, in a strictly scientific sense. Science is demonstrated truth—actual knowledge. Strictly, science is based on
known facts and principles, which are used theoretically to
deduce other facts and principles. Hypothesis assumes facts
and principles and on that proceeds to deduction. If we
assume the biblical history to be true, to be a revelation to
man by God, we have assumed facts to build on and thence
deduce conclusions and build up theology. If we look upon
the works of nature, see a design, believe there must have
been a designer, and believe that designer to be God, we
assume there is a God, and from known facts and principles in
connection with Nature seek to deduce a scientific demonstration. Both foundations are based on faith, one sustained by
revelation, taken as such by faith, the other on the hypothesis
that there is a designer and he must be God.

A theory may be founded on facts that agree with it and be
deductively established. It is a theory because it agrees with
its environment. Theology is purely a deductive science.
All theories formed must be based on hypothesis. No real
induction can be applied to it. The nearest we can come to
known facts on which to base a theory is, by assuming that a
consciousness attends on every sane intelligent mind, that
there is an intelligence somewhere, higher than our own, and
as there are forces in nature that operate as if guided by
intelligence, that are infinite in power compared with any we
can produce, their origin and end unknown to us and it is

beyond our ability to ascertain, therefore, they are created
by an infinite intelligence which exists.

Theologians confound theology, religion and Christianity.
Theology, confounded with religion and called Christianity, is
brought into the prison question, and occupies a large field in
the views and efforts to regulate prisons, prescribe punishment
and effect reforms in convicts. An extended examination of
the subject is imperative, and in the space permitted here it
must be somewhat discursive. There is no design to prove or
disprove the existence of a Deity, but to treat of the subject
as a factor in the prison question.

Man sees the exhibitions of force in nature around him
beyond his strength, and beyond his comprehension as to its
cause. He connects it with the existence of a personal power
and stands in fear of it. This is a fact applying to all races of
men.

Next, there is a desire to live somewhere after death here.
Man connects space and the universe of matter as far as he
can see and comprehend it with that Being, and from that come
his ideas of eternity, or what he calls endless time compared
with life here. That desire to live hereafter, and the fear of
this unknown and incomprehensible Being of his own creation,
bring acts which we call worship; and this is also common to
all races in some form, visible or invisible. The two together
—the ideas formed of the relation to that Being and the ideas
as to the proper way to recognize the existence of and treat
that Being in thought and act, with a view to secure through
Him life beyond the grave, make up in each person what we
call religion; and on this, like minds get together in groups
or "religious congregations."

Some minds find no place where they can rest; no set of
ideas with which they are content; speculation, doubt and
change of opinions affect them from time to time; hence, the
great numbers of creeds, and religions and modes of worship
on one hand, and so-called atheism, agnosticism and materialism on the other. Those easily satisfied are the religious
optimists. Those dissatisfied are the pessimists.

Who and what this Being is, where He is, how He works,
and all that relates to Him and His attributes is called

theology — the science of God. It is founded on opinion, and that opinion is itself founded on opinion ; thus—opinion first that such a Being exists as a personal Being, and next, opinion as to what He is and His attributes, our relations, duties, etc. This, like an inference from an inference, proves nothing positively, while an inference from a fact may have the force of fact. If a man be found dead with the marks of a left hand on his left hand, we may infer they were made by some other person than himself, because it is an inference from a fact ; but we could not infer that they were made by any particular person who had a left hand, that being only an inference from an inference. Science deals with facts. If, from what we know, we form an opinion, and by facts can inductively establish it, we may infer other facts deductively from that opinion.

I said God exists as a personal Being to those who believe in Him, because the attempt to comprehend this Being as a "spirit, without body, parts or passions" amounts to verbiage only. Man cannot conceive of an active intelligence without a form, and he cannot conceive of a form higher than his own. Nor can he conceive of this Being called God without giving Him human attributes—calling them infinite, without limit, because he cannot conceive of any intelligence higher than his own. Therefore, whether admitted or not, God, to every person who thinks of Him, is a personal Being.

Strictly speaking, Christianity in practice has nothing to do with either theology or religion. Jesus Christ was a person who laid down certain rules to live by. He promised eternal life to those who observed those rules and adopted them in practice in their intercourse with their fellow-man. Before his time the kingdom of force had existed as the rule : "An eye for an eye, and a tooth for a tooth." He taught that the true rule was to live as a brotherhood. He told of a kingdom of Heaven, but it began on earth by building up a kingdom of love in each soul in place of a kingdom of force. For disciples who were to promulgate these new rules of life, He required them to add the practice of non-resistance ; and for all men to do as they would like to be done by under the same circumstances. He gave many instructions to His chosen disciples that were not intended for mankind generally, but modern theology treats them as if addressed to each individual. The most enlightened person, the most ignorant one, the semi-civilized or the barbarian must be wiser, better and happier, the nearer his life is guided by these rules. This kind of life would ensure another life hereafter, in the presence of a Superior Being. To those who believed and practiced it it could be called a religion; but if a man was an atheist and practiced these rules he would be a Christian. A practice of them and not simply a belief in them constitutes Christianity. The theologian gives Christ divine attributes and so seeks to make Christianity a part of theology; while a man may be practically a Christian who never heard of Christ.

The universe of matter operates and moves by reaction. All progress is in reaction. Natural laws are uniform and maintain equilibrium. Certain elements make an acid, others make an alkali. United in certain proportions, they combine, neutralize each other, part escapes in gas, and the residue forms a neutral salt, each a base for future combinations. Nothing is lost. All progress is permanent, whether toward a higher or lower plane and until new forces change conditions. Intellectual progress upward or downward, forms no exception; what is gained in one direction is lost in another, constant change and constant re-adjustment making up the sum of evolution, and it is constant and eternal throughout the universe.

Neither scientist or savage is or can be free from the consciousness of force in nature superior to all he knows or can imagine. As far as we go down with the microscope we find perfect organization, adaptation and fixed laws. When we come up to ourselves in the range of animal life, we reach the end of investigation. We can find nothing higher or more perfect. We meet the mysteries of life and death all through our search, from lowest to highest, and we cannot solve those mysteries. We go out into space with the telescope, the spectroscope and the camera, and as far as we can get we find perfect order, perfect law, and, so far as we can discover, the same elements, causes and effects we find here. We could not discover any other if they existed, because we cannot know any other only as we discover and learn them here. For all we know, the range of life may go on upward to infinity after it passes us and our knowledge. The air and space may be filled with beings we cannot discover and know in our present condition—proceeding upward in intelligence and power, in regular gradation, as life proceeds from the protoplasm to us. Or, from aught we know, a new series of strata, or an ascending grade may begin of aerial, ethereal life, each fitted to its sphere; and there may be a plane on which our own intelligent energy may live and act hereafter. In time, communication may take place between us and that plane above. While to our finite perceptions the probabilities of it may seem about equal to intelligent communication between the protoplasmic forms and ourselves, it is not impossible that a higher plane exists for our own intelligence in another form, and that mediums of communication may exist, as we see them in material existence, and designate them by the name of "substantial immaterial force." While in my opinion there can be no such thing as an immaterial force—as I shall try to demonstrate hereafter—I use the definition to convey the idea of the invisible and as yet unknowable.

I repeat that plane after plane, and stage after stage of life and intelligence may exist, almost infinitely, and there may be one Being in some form at the head, co-existent and consistent with it all, as we find beings co-existent and consistent with each plane as far as our knowledge of life reaches. But we are left to imagination and speculation when we try to pass beyond ourselves and the boundaries of our own knowledge.

We see perfect design and we may say there can be no design without a designer; but in that design we find no two things alike. There is eternal and unexceptional variation as far as knowledge takes us. We find universal force and we may say it always existed. Who can deny it other than by assertion? Passing beyond ourselves and left to imagination and speculation, surrounded by active life of which we are a part, we see that life cease and decomposition follow in some of those around us. The longing to live, to resurrect that life, to be once more active, carries the imagination out into space as far as we can go, and we people it somewhere with a new life; always human in form, always human in action, always clothed with exalted human attributes; always coming back to us because we are in doubt and want proof—tangible proof—that it is there. The insoluble mystery of life, the intangibility of thought, the invisibility of mind, are seized on as means to create proofs and we form an opinion. One dreams, and to his mind it is evidence and with him opinion becomes belief. Another looks on a cataleptic, who seems to see through the skull and describes things at a distance correctly, as he would see through a glass and describe things present, and to him it is proof of the supernatural, and his opinion becomes belief in the supernatural. Another sees or hears things he cannot comprehend, and to him they are supernatural and he forms an opinion, and without other evidence than want of explanation he calls his opinion belief.

Great learning and powers of reasoning never exist in perfection in any person. Limited boundaries of knowledge and narrow powers of reasoning exist in the large majority of mankind. Weak places exist somewhere in every intellect, and they are filled by means as various as are the situations of men. A learned lawyer may believe in ghosts, or visible spirits, as in the case of Judge Edmunds and Robert Dale Owen. A great scientist may dread to upset his salt dish. A profound philosopher may be afraid to ride on a railroad or to start on a journey on Friday. These weak places are filled to a greater or less extent by impressions created by the surroundings of the individual and from sources he has no hand in making. He does not form his own brain at first, or supply the food that makes nerve and brain matter, nor teach himself his first ideas, nor acquire by his own efforts his first knowledge of facts. The impressions made on him by his early environment and teaching are never wholly eradicated. The impressions made about God, religion, and future existence are inseparable from his after life, no matter what conclusion he finally reaches.

The filling of these waste or weak places—those not filled and hardened by knowledge of actual facts after the individual becomes matured—constitutes the opinions and beliefs making up the various religions, denominations and creeds, and the various grades of belief among spiritualists. These places are the lodging places of superstition. Among the great mass they are large and numerous. Among the learned they are less so or less crude. Among the scientific they may not be obtrusive, but they exist—and certainly as the homes of doubt if no more.

A child is born and is a mere animal without mind. It grows and is taught, and with knowledge of things coming through the senses comes mind. It reaches manhood and dies, and the mind seems to die with it, so far as we can see here. What was the mind? That has been the inquiry of mankind from the earliest dawn of history. All we know is, it came with growth of the body and knowledge acquired through the bodily senses, and it had no cognizance of anything beyond that. Was it the seed or germ to create a new mind to be perfected somewhere else, or was it a part of the universal energy converted into mind force by the operations of matter, as demonstrated through the physical organisms of the human body? We don't know. But in experience we find innumerable cases where mind meets mind, and mind matter—so to speak—in different persons mingles together. A few years ago in Pennsylvania, a farmer sent his son on a two days' journey to a city, with a team, some property, and money. On the night of the day he started, the farmer dreamed that the son was attacked at a place he saw in his dream, but had not seen before, was robbed, and called to him for help. He awoke, and was so impressed that he took to the road and followed on, and at the end of his first day's journey he came to the place and found the place and the facts as he had seen them in his dream.

Recently, in Iowa, a lady dreamed that an accident had happened to her sister who was in Hot Springs, Arkansas. She saw the party present, carriages, horses and surroundings, but had never been there. She wrote to her sister, giving details and description in full. She had never seen the persons or places. The accident happened exactly as she described it as to persons, places and results.

I am sitting in my room. Some one I have no reason to expect appears to my mind to be coming, to be at the gate ; and presently the door opens and they enter. I feel it all and yet there was nothing I know of to make me think they were

coming. Like cases are common to most persons. People
foretell close coming events in which the elements are already
at work, and not by process of reasoning. Loss of life at sea,
and death in battle, are known to others hundreds of miles
away at the time they occur.

Mind has certain sympathies and repulsions, or, when acted
on attracts or repels; as if it were material and its atoms acted
on other mind atoms, under certain conditions. Its phenomena
being seen, and being apparently unexplainable, and not being understood, the imagination, tempered by former impressions lying in these places not filled by actual knowledge, to
which I have alluded, soars away into the regions of the supernatural to find a solution, and closes on all it sees that is unexplainable as evidence that the mind is a deathless soul, that it
will have life hereafter; that there is another world for us and
a great personal ruler; and it rests in content in a hope of
that life.

It is said of Orestes A. Brownson—a man of brains and fine
literary acquirements—that he went the round of the Protestant churches and beliefs, listening, reading, reasoning and spec-
ulating, and longing for rest, but found none. He dropped into
the Roman Catholic church and let that think for him, and
died in peace. Why? Because it was a systematic belief, practical and material in all of its details of outward observance,
mysterious enough in its symbolisms to satisfy his curiosity,
and had a perfect government, all of which harmonized with
his peculiar mentality. Another mind, equally wise but differently developed, takes what contented him—the Catholic faith
—as evidence of bigoted tyranny and bloodthirsty intolerance.

All religious beliefs are intolerant. No religion can exist
unless it be intolerant. A man forms an opinion and sends the
imagination into the realms of the mysterious for evidence,
finds something that coincides with his opinion, takes it as evidence and so forms a belief. His mentality—that is, his mental
organization and the impressions made upon it—develops such
perceptions as cause him to see and accept that something as
evidence, and this belief becomes the mentalism—or outgrowth
—of those perceptions. Others of like mentalism unite with
him. They confirm themselves in the conclusion that they are

right. They reject all that disproves their conclusion. They become impatient of question and will not tolerate contradiction. Unlike scientists, they search for all that will sustain them and ignore all that refutes them. Christianity comes in and teaches charity, the law prohibits force, and the variety of beliefs—all combined—prevent intolerance from becoming aggressive. The Protestant churches on one side divided into many congregations, are held in balance by the Roman Catholic united as a whole under a perfect government on the other, and toleration exists between. But each fails to find rest for all who unite with them severally; and the wanderers, those who fail to find rest, organize schisms and secessions, form new opinions, and new beliefs spring up. For others spiritism and free love afford a rest; for others still, materialism and agnosticism and atheism afford temporary content. What looks like evidence to one mind is none at all to another. The degree of intelligence or social position of the believers have little to do with it. All depends on the mentality, and that depends on the mental organization and the impressions that have been made upon it. Ignorance will seize on a desirable hope where intelligence will pause to inquire; but in emotional temperaments both alike will follow a pleasing idea without inquiry. Vice will adopt a belief that offers a chance for progress hereafter without restraint here, that intelligence or ascetic morality will reject as inconsistent with justice. An intelligent person who is of an emotional nature and given to the marvelous may be as prone to superstitions as ignorance itself, and yield to some of them against reason and better knowledge. The nervous and the sanguine will seize on a comfortable and easy belief, while the ascetic and the sceptical will reject it because it is so.

The constant widening of the field of scientific discovery has changed the views of many theologians, and to-day the sermons of the Rev. Lyman Beecher would not find a ready response in one of the congregations that hung delighted on the utterances of his son, the late Henry Ward Beecher. The communicants and churchgoers include a minority only of the people, and of these a majority are females. Of the numbers that come under prison restraint but few ever attend religious service, and for them theology has no attractions. With those who fall from good position to the place of convicts—and it includes some of high intelligence and religious profession—all theological learning and influence have failed as a restraining force; and where not worn by them as a cloak to hide evil designs, it has made no impressions with strength sufficient to counteract temptation. In other words, the moral governing force was not adapted tó the animal motive power and intellectual working machinery; and if again sought to be used as a governor by stimulating into activity in the prison, will be likely to again prove its want of adaptation; either from want of acuteness of moral perception, or the overbearing force of the animal impulses. (The reader must not construe this word "animal" impulses to refer alone to the idea of sex. It refers to personal gratification in any respect other than intellectual: personal desires, wants, pride, ambition, appetites.) If the mentality of the individual is of such a character that the deductions of theologians as presented in the prisons take hold of the mind of the convict and build up a hope through and fear of God as to a life hereafter, and the impressions made are such as become permanent, as a factor in reform theology will aid in strengthening the moral force as a regulating part of the mental machinery. Otherwise, it will be lost labor. It is plain to be seen that, a body of men and women in prison are not mentally different from the same persons out. Socially, there is this difference and no other: in prison they can be corraled and made to listen, which cannot be done outside. But how effectually they can be reached by theological teaching and discussion, in view of all the facts as they exist, is a problem that can be solved only by individual experiment. As a whole it is insoluble. Reasoning from analogy, we might be justified in believing it would be no more effectual in prison than it is out.

As commonly understood, it is a misnomer to speak of the convicts as "the crime class." Convicts come from every class among men; and many come from among those who are well-to-do in the world, who have such advantages as would enable them to live respectable and honest. Crime in a mental sense exists among all classes, as disease does in a physical sense.

When we carry theology and its teachings into the prisons we enter among people in no wise different—so far as the outcome of its influence is concerned—from those in the community outside, except that the prisoners are under restraint and discipline while those outside are not.

It cannot be denied that, up to this time in this country, the church takes the place of a standing army in preserving public order. It opens an outlet for the emotional impulses, and the zeal of a certain portion of the people, who, but for that outlet would find others, requiring physical force to keep them in order. There is an element in all animal life—more active in man because of his intelligence—seldom noticed and rarely if ever considered. That is, a constant craving for artificial excitement—that is to say, some created excitement; something that does not arise in the ordinary channels of every-day life. We see it in force in young animals—the kittens, the dogs, the coyotes, foxes, and all others. You may place a baby on the floor and surround it with all kinds of means for amusement, and it will leave them and crawl off after something else. You may make home among a family of children as attractive as it can be, and devise evening amusements, and the youths in it will slip off and go out to hunt something else. There is no place in life where this craving does not exist, and human animals would be non-progressive without it. With mankind, as age creeps on, this craving increases as the years approach and enter on the stage of manhood, and it depends entirely on the mental and physical formation and the individual environment what character it will assume in seeking gratification and in manifestations. Its progress, changes, and ultimate developments will depend on the material surroundings. In all cases it will cling to that which affords the most ready and congenial gratification, that most in harmony with the mental impulses. The outlet may be morbid, or vicious, or reckless, or benevolent, and it develops in endless forms. The missionary, the sister of charity, the voluntary manager of orphans' homes, kindergartens, refuges for abandoned women, etc., find their excitement there. The trapper, pioneer, scout, adventurer and explorer find theirs in the wilds. The believer in the spiritual and supernatural will revel in ghost stories, and shudder over the mysterious and horrible. The revivalist preacher, who can drive people wild with emotional hope and fear, and the people he affects, are only types of men and women who, under different environment in early life, and under other influences, would fall into the excitement of drink, gossip, narcotics, and various kinds of crime. Some have done so, and will again.

This craving is universal in all animal life. The elephant's trunk is never still, and the unruly cow breaks through all enclosures. Of those among mankind needing restraint, beginning with the one who gets drunk, and is otherwise harmless, and going on to the one who deliberately steals or murders on the vicious plane, or beginning with the theological enthusiast and going on to the radical reformer and the bigotry that burned John Rogers and Servetus, on the so-called moral plane, it is always present, ever active, always outward in all phases of life. The theologian, looking to the origin, calls it "man's inherent depravity." It is immaterial what we call it, while it it very material that we recognize it as a serious fact in considering the prison question.

The churches afford an outlet for this craving to a minority; and but for that, garrisons of soldiers would be required to preserve public order. Of the majority the larger part are kept in order by an innate love of order, and some by selfish considerations, from fear as to person and property, with no care otherwise. Some fear the law and its penalties, and so keep order while no other idea specially restrains them.

Theology ignores these facts more or less when it comes to practice. It says to all: "You must believe in God and worship Him, or there is no chance for you to abandon crime life and live on a moral or orderly plane." Of course, that will influence only such as have the kind of mind that conceives of this God and the impulses to believe in and worship Him. That being only the minority, as an element for reform in the prison question, its field of action is limited, and in the end other influences must be relied on to control, reform and dispose of convicts. With physical force we can accept the aid of the theologian, but theologians themselves must enlarge their views, and recognize the fact, that were their methods and

ideas alone to be carried into practice there would be a failure.
There is no middle ground with theology. When persuasion
fails there is no power left, except the thumb-screws and the
guillotine. A man who does not understand your language
cannot respond to you. A man whose mentality cannot grasp
your theological conclusions can have neither opinion nor
belief in harmony with them. If he cannot grasp any theological view he is a born materialist and cannot be influenced by
anything theology can give him, unless his mentality can be so
changed by education as to bring into activity the latent
elements that will seek an outlet through the supernatural,
the combination of brain ganglia that brings reverence, benevolence, conscientiousness, love of approbation, self-esteem, hope,
marvelousness and fear of the unknown acting together as a
moral force.

Whatever may be urged before us that is incomprehensible
by us as presented, we are compelled to shape, measure and
make perceptible by forms and comparisons of and with which
we have knowledge through the senses. No one mind can
form or shape an image and describe it in words so another
mind can mentally see and comprehend it exactly as it appears
to the mind that creates or describes it. For this reason there
can be no absolutely fixed standard of right and wrong. All
standards are arbitrary and temporary. Each age and each
nation and community has its own ; they are not alike, and are
constantly changing. The theologian erects a standard called
conscience and declares it to be a supernatural perception
coming from God, inherent in each person. Experience
teaches us that this conscience is only a human conclusion
depending on the perception of the individual, and his perception depends on his brains, his environment and his education.
Even the believers in conscience are not able to adhere to it
and guide all their actions by it alike, and are constantly
changing it. As yet, superstition—measured by this standard
—is as necessary to control some minds as strong walls are to
control some bodies. "What a man loves, that he wills to do,"
says Swedenborg. In fact, a man's acts are governed by his
opinions, and his opinions are the outgrowth of his mentality and environment, and they are dependent on conditions

over which he has no control in his earlier life. The standards
of Talmadge, or Ingersoll, or Victoria Woodhull would not
have been listened to a century ago. Now they command
large audiences. Such is the difference in that decade and
this one. The Mosaic standard was repudiated by Christ—
saying he came to fulfill the law. The *lex talionis* had been
the rule. For this he laid down the law of brotherhood and
forgiveness. The radical Mohamedan is right in his conscience
when he slays a hated Gaiour, and the cannibal king is right in
his when he knocks a fat young native in the head and presents the carcass to you for your dinner, as the highest
compliment he can pay you. By the Christian conscience
both would be murderers. The Episcopalian priest will preach
in no pulpit except that of his own church. The Roman
Catholic says he is no priest. The ancient Roman took the
life of his wife, child or servant at his pleasure. His successor
declares it murder. It is not long since we hung the man who
killed the seducer of his wife; to-day, while the statute
remains unchanged, the standard as held up in the jury-box
condemns the statute and approves the killing. Seventy years
ago the preacher kept a bottle convenient and refreshed
himself with a dram after his three hours' service in the pulpit;
to-day the service and the bottle would not be permitted. It
is useless to multiply instances, the truth is patent to the most
casual observer.

Because of the absence of any fixed standard, and because
of the different standards and the continual changes in them,
much indifference exists in the minds of those criminally
inclined as to any consideration of right or wrong; and the
most of them hold the law and its penalties in more or less
contempt so far as they are proposed as a means of moral
reform, because of the uncertainty and inequality as to infliction of penalties. And, again, when they see the law itself
perpetrating injustice in various ways; for instance, permitting
wholesale gambling on the board of trade while a wager on
cards or billiards is made a crime; or in robbery by corporations and the conspiracy of combines, while deceit and oppression by individuals is punished as criminal; the evils and
robbery from legislation in favor of one class and against all

others, while false pretenses by a person is made felony; and in many other ways that can be named; they take a sort of pride in defying the law, and exult in every successful effort to defeat it. As long as such conditions exist, the foothold for theological influence, as a means to effect reform of convicts, will be extremely narrow.

The Jewish history, as recorded in the Bible is a theological history. The theologians, claiming to be inspired directly by God Himself, speaking as His ministers and inspired prophets, labored for hundreds of years to establish and maintain order and morality. But the people divided, and vacillated and alternated in adherence to one of two gods, Yahweh (Jehovah) and Baal, and finally went to destruction as a nation. They were scattered over the whole known world, a people without a country, and became the persecuted of all nations, countries and peoples. Adhering to certain of the laws their theologians had given them, they dwindled and diminished in numbers until they counted not over, or less, than five millions of people. It was not until the civilization that followed the overturning of the domination of priestcraft under the Christian faith, and the reformation in the Jewish laws relating to purification, that the Jews began to increase in numbers, and in the western nations of Europe to be accorded civil rights. All modern theology is based on this history, deriving whatever inspiration or authority it claims from it; the Christian theologians having entered the Jewish tabernacles and appropriated it, and added to it the New Testament of Christian faith and history; and for over eighteen centuries have forced it through the various changes, as did their Jewish predecessors, until the present theology is the result.

Are we not justified in concluding, then, that in dealing with mankind as a factor in government, it is available so far as the mentality of men find its teachings acceptable to their perceptions and responsive to their longings; and beyond that it is of no avail? If so, then it must be addressed to such, and the claim that there can be no reform without it is a claim that cannot be substantiated, nor can it be admitted to the exclusion—or obstruction, even—of other methods for reform, and the building up of the mentality that will comprehend the

necessity for and the duty to observe public order.   With or
without the Christian theology, associated man must have and
submit to government, and there are only two kinds: One,
civil, based on order ; one, turbulent, based on anarchy.   In
the first that theology can exist as one feature because there is
protection for its adherents.   In the other it cannot, only as
Christian believers among the turbulent may gain temporary
ascendency.

CHAPTER V.

MIND.

I HAVE made some references to this subject in the preceding chapter, but I deem it of importance to treat it separately and more fully. For the purposes contemplated in this work I will pass by the recognized premises and deductions of scientists as to what mind is, and assume a position as a point for illustration.

Mind is supposed to be impressions made on the gray matter in the brain—and probably involving the whole nervous system with the natural senses. Without the senses and impressions made through them there is no mind. The animal body may exist and perform the functions to sustain life without other consciousness than that in the different organs and particles of matter in the body, which must have conscious intelligence of their own to perform the several functions allotted to them without confusion. For comparison we may designate this as the physiological or animal mind, while we call the mind proper the intellectual mind. Both are an entity, an impulse, an energy, a force; born of matter, a result of matter in motion; existing only in and with matter, acting on and being acted on only by and through matter. When we step before a mirror the light impresses our image on it, and reflects it back to us again, but it does not retain the impression. If we should coat the mirror with a sensitized coating and reflect the image on it, it would retain the image for a time. If we should add another coating for the purpose, it would retain the image permanently. So with what is called the sensorium. Impressions made upon the senses of sight, hearing, smell, taste and feeling are sometimes merely impressed for the moment and disappear, like that on the mirror. Others remain for a time and then fade away. Others become permanent and we call it memory. Again, sometimes a fixed impression on a plate fades, and a new coating of the right chemical will restore it. So the impression on the memory may fade; and by exercise of mental force we can recall it— recollect, as we say—and restore it to the memory. Like the diamond that absorbs and reflects light, when laid away a long time in darkness will lose its light, but if dipped into warm water will again show light as if lying latent in it and is recalled by the warm fluid.

Just where these impressions are made, how they are made, what they are made on or in, how they are retained, or recalled when lost for the time, or what the character of the energy or force is, is not known. Like other subtle and invisible things, we can only see the results of its action in some cases, and from that form an opinion. The natural senses may all be active and there be no mind, from absence of intellectual brain, or defective quality or arrangement of brain matter.

While brain has one general character, it differs in texture, quality of tissue, sensibility to impressions, quickness of response in impulse caused by impressions, and in arrangement of vital centers, as well as in volume. Among the hundreds of millions there are no two exactly alike.

Mind is the receptacle as well as result of such impressions as are made on the body through the natural senses, and the impulses created by those impressions. There is first an impression on the sense from the action of matter outside of the body; that impression is carried to the sensorium through the nerves, and impresses itself and becomes conscious knowledge. The outside impression ceases and the sensorium retains that impression as knowledge, and from it comes an impulse called thought, and that thought goes out and takes cognizance of the matter that made the impression. Continued impressions on all of the senses from endless action of matter outside, and continued impulses as thoughts resulting from the impressions, with impulses from the operations of accumulated and combined thought, make mind. The impressions and impulses will depend on the peculiar character and formation of the brain, or whatever makes up the sensorium on which the impression is made.

(We begin to make impressions on the convict, and the impression he may receive may not be the one we intend to make, and the impulse—thought—that results will be such as *his* mind, not *ours*, will produce. If we understand his mind we can better calculate the impression he will receive and the result from it—producing thought in him, and so affecting his mind in producing new mind.)

If I take a silver coin and lay it on the top of my tongue, and a copper one and put it under my tongue, and bring the edges together over the end of my tongue, the salt and acid in the fluid secretions of the mouth will begin to corrode the metal in the coins—that is, make an impression on them. From that impression an impulse will start that we call electric force, or energy, as the thought starts from the mental impression. It will pass from one coin to the other, through the tongue, back onto the coins again in a circuit; and it will continue as long as I keep the edges together—that is, as long as the impression of the fluids continues on the coins; just as an impression on the eye will go to the brain, create the impulse of thought and come back through the eye and note what caused the impression, and continue while the impression lasts. When I separate the edges the impulse will cease. If I bring them together again the impulse will start again. Just so will the eye carry an impulse to and from the brain as long as impressions continue. The impulse will create a stinging impression on the tongue, and there will be a metallic taste in the mouth. Here are two impressions—feeling and taste—that are made on the sensorium through those senses, and an impulse starts there as thought and continues as long as the tongue stings and the mouth tastes. The coins retain the marks of the corrosion (although they may not be visible to us), that is, the impression made on them by the fluids of the mouth, as the sensorium retains the impression made by the senses; and there has been a consumption of brain tissue in the mental action as there has been of the metal in the electric action. The current disappears, as the thought does, as soon as the impression ceases. The sensorium is sentient and can recall the thought whenever some other impression prompts an impulse of like character, as the coin recalls it on the edges being brought together. Whether the coins are sentient and can recall the impressions made on them is beyond our comprehension; but here were two forces in the action of matter in immediate contact, dependent on and growing out of each other, born of action and re-action in matter—electric force and mind-force—both properties of and in matter, and alike in modes of action. The one remains with us, the other disappears but leaves with us knowledge of it, and we can recall it with the coins at our pleasure, a mechanical act. We do it by an impulse of the mind-force. Whether that is a mechanical act or not we do know, but we do know there is a consumption of brain tissue with every mental impulse, as there is consumption of the metals with the electric impulse, and we cannot be contradicted if we say it was mechanical—dictated by the conscious intelligence in the matter constituting the sensorium.

I can create this electric force at pleasure and give it conductors, and convey impressions, and create mind-force with it a thousand miles and more away. I will suspend a plate of zinc and one of copper in each of two jars of acid, and with two wires connect the zincs in each jar with the coppers in the other, keeping the plates separated. The metals will begin to corrode (oxidize) and the electric force will start, run from the metal in one jar to the metal in the other, over the wire, through the acid onto the other metal, back on the other wire to the other plate in the first jar, through the acid onto the first plate, in a circuit, and continue as long as the corrosion of the metals goes on and I leave the wires attached. Now, if one jar is here and another in New York, and one wire between, I can put the ends of the other wire down into the moist earth, and the earth will complete the circuit as well as a second wire would do if carried clear through. If, before carrying the wire to New York (or anywhere between the jars), I wind it around a piece of soft iron, the current, in passing around the iron, will make an impression on it from which a new impulse will start called magnetic force, and the iron will become a magnet and attract steel. If I cut off the current by detaching the wire the magnetic force will disappear with the electric force and the iron will cease to be a magnet. It does not retain the impression—it has forgotten. But I can recall it again by attaching the wire and starting the electric current. If I substitute a piece of iron charged with carbon—that is, steel—and send the current around it, it will become a magnet and will retain the impression and be a permanent magnet. It will remember. This electric force will not start unless it can make a circuit and get back again. Here the metals and acid correspond with the action in matter outside of the body, and the wire corresponds with the sensitory nerve that conveys the impression to the sensorium. The iron corresponds with the sensorium that receives the impression, and the magnetic force takes the place of the thought the impression generates, and then forgets. The magnetic force on the steel takes the place of the thought that is generated, and remembers. And the mind-force, like the electric force, will not start unless it can complete a circuit. Unless the body, nerve and sensorium, are in such condition that the outside action will make an impression and create thought, and the thought takes conscious notice of what made the impression—flows back to the start—there will be no mind-force. The decomposition of the metals in the acid corresponds with the consumption of brain and nerve tissue; and as the acid and metals must be renewed, so the tissue must be replaced by nutrition. The analogy is complete throughout. If I place a small metal bar on a pivot over this magnet and send the current through that, as often as it touches the magnet the current will start on the circuit, and when I remove it from the magnet it will stop. In this way by dots and dashes, or variant sounds, representing letters, I can write, just as the mind-force, going to the hand, can express the thoughts from the impressions with a pen.

From the principle of the telegraph let us turn to the phonograph. Every tone in sound produces its own peculiar vibration in the surrounding medium, and that vibration brings into action electric force. If we take a cylinder having a small spiral groove running around it, and cover it with thin foil, place it in front of and close to a small metal point attached to a diaphragm, so that the point comes over the groove, and arrange the cylinder with clock-work so it will revolve and move forward, keeping the groove close and opposite to the point, and then make sounds so the vibrations can reach the diaphragm, the same vibrations in the surrounding medium will be communicated to the diaphragm, and the point will in-dent the foil with the number of dents, of proper depth and length, corresponding to the number force and duration of the vibrations made by each tone of sound. If the cylin-der be then put back, starting at the beginning, and be turned as before, as the little point passes over the indentations in the foil, it will vibrate the diaphragm; that will give the same vibrations to the surrounding medium, generate electric force and the same tones will be carried to the ear and im-pressed on the sensorium; thought is produced, and we think we hear the same tones that were made in the ear or re-ceiver of the phonograph. Here the electric force—every-where present in matter—is generated, not by the decomposi-tion of metals, but by the vibrations of the ether, (and perhaps air) or whatever constitutes the surrounding medium in space. (The *air* wave theory of sound is not accepted.)

Now, the particles in the body are never still—all is in vibra-tory motion in some form. Decomposition of matter never ceases, but waste of tissue (and its conversion into water, carried off through the skin, lungs and kidneys,) is constant, and supply of more through digestion and assimilation of food goes on, as long as the machinery lasts; just as the elec-tric force goes on as long as the materials last. Does this pro-cess in the human system generate electric force? Is the hu-man organism an electrical machine, complete in itself, as long as the materials last, or until the circuit is broken by de-struction of the battery or the wires (the sensorium and nerves), or of the jars and wasting of acids, (the body and blood), or the complete corrosion of the metals, (the whole cell structure of the body)? Does it produce the electric force in all forms, and manifestations, and methods? We take a dy-namo and generate the electric force, and store it up in plates and pack them away as the mind does thoughts—knowledge. We detach the steam power from the engine that runs the dy-namo, and attach the plates, so as to make a circuit on an elec-tric motor, and the stored electric force in the plates runs the dynamo to generate more electricity, just as the mind force stored up in the brain plates, in the form of knowledge, uses that knowledge to generate more impressions, and create more knowledge. All that comes of knowledge is changes in the forms of matter through the action of the person. Is the human organism one form of dynamo, generating electric force, and storing it up in the sensorium plates, to be used in turn to run the dynamos, to generate more force; and within it the telegraph, the telephone, the phonograph, the electric clock, the electric motor, and all the uses to which that force can be put, and many others as yet unknown, perhaps as infinite as the the universe?

Several electric currents can be sent over the same circuit conductor, in different directions at the same time, conveying different messages; just as several impressions can be conveyed over the nerves to the sensorium at the same time, generating different thoughts, and leaving different knowledge; as in eating a rich, fragrant apple, while talking about it, every sense—eye, ear, smell, taste and feeling—all are impressed at once. And there is a further force, a compound of the animal and intellectual minds, generating a sense or impression of gratification, enjoyment, pleasure; just as there is in the triumph of duplex telegraphy, less the gastronomic sense. Is mind force one of the productions of the action of electric force in matter, as magnetic force is?

What is the visible reaction of this mind force? Simply changes in the form of matter from the mechanical acts of the human body, directed by these thoughts—this knowledge obtained from impressions made by matter. Houses, books, machinery, ships, railroads, farms, forms of food and raiment, statutes, cathedrals, statuary, monuments—and all the creations of humanity in the use of knowledge, each making more impression and generating more thought and knowledge in combined thoughts. The pen that wrote Magna Charta and the axe that beheaded Charles the First; the emancipation proclamation and the gallows that hung Guiteau; the comic valentine and the Angelus; the patent medicine almanac and Newton's Principia; the jumping-jack to impress the child and the Lick telescope to confound scientists with the revelation of the nebulæ. Such uses as create impressions that form the mind of the criminal; make his acts crimes; bring about his conviction; builds the prison that receives him; the mind that there seeks to control his mind and by new impressions substitute in him another mind; the force moves in a circuit, from matter, through the force it generates in one form, to matter in another form. The force that makes mind is clearly a material force, and the mind force in turn manifests itself in a material way, leaving that evidence that it also is a material force. I need not pursue this subject further for the purpose I intend it to serve, which will be seen further on. As an illustration of the generation of invisible energy, this principle of the electric telgraph and phonograph is an exact illustration of the generation of mind force on another plane—that of animal intelligence.

The experience of every day demonstrates that, somewhere in nature there are elements that establish circuits in which the mind force moves and acts in connection with other mind force in other persons; it may be a short or a long distance away. At certain times and under certain conditions the mind force in one person is conveyed to, and operates on the mind force in another person, and we designate it as psychic force; (soul force—psychology being a discourse about the soul; a deductive soul science, like theology); just as if one brain or sensorium was a battery here, and another brain or sensorium was another battery somewhere else, and in some way in the action of the elements in matter, a conductor is established between them like the wire between the jars, and some action in the two bodies starts a current and communication takes place between them. Impressions are conveyed and felt, and intelligent action follows from thought created by the impressions. I have alluded to it, but we may specially note that when the decomposition of the metal ceases the electric force ceases; and when the wire is detached it does not pass. Just so with the mind. If the sensorial nerve loses its vitality no impression is conveyed. Or if there be unconsciousness none is received, though the nerve be normal; and in either case there is no creation of mind. And though there may be consciousness, yet if from disease there be no impression there will be no mind force as to the part affected by disease, as in deafness, loss of smell, etc. Disintegration of tissue goes on during sleep and suspended animation, but not as when awake and under mental stimulus; but in cases of partial suspension of animation there may be mental action while the power of motion is dormant, as in catalepsy, or when under the power of hypnosis. The same thing applies to conductors between two mind forces. There is no circuit and no impression unless brain and nerve are in condition to receive and produce impressions. There are conditions when impressions can be received during partial sleep, when there are dreams, and which admit of as rational explanation, as do those when the mind is wholly awake.

In reference to the conductors between different minds, let us consider a somnambulist briefly. Take a sleep-walker who has had impressions made on him from birth to manhood, and the action and reaction of mind force has created mind with general and varied knowledge. The intellect is asleep, but the animal mind is carrying on all of the bodily functions. Something disturbs this action and partially arouses the intellectual mind force and there the disturbance is suspended, but leaves the newly aroused impulse active. The sleeper's partially aroused mind prompts some action, goes ahead leading the way, and the body—unconscious of all else around it—follows. There is more or less of the force that exists in catalepsy, for no impression is made on the sensorium from outside objects other than the one that roused the sleeper, and on which the mind force is suspended. The body has no sense of feeling in a natural way. The feet do not feel when they touch the floor so as to convey any conscious impression to the sensorium. The sleeper will walk out of a high door or window or off of the roof of a house as if walking on a level. The body follows the impulse of the partially aroused force until the force has spent itself, and remains unconscious otherwise. No impression is made on the sensorium that remains, and there is no memory of the act. If he be aroused the mind immediately connects itself with the matter around him, and receives impressions through the senses from it; but there is no knowledge from the sleep-walking act. Was this an exhibition of latent psychic force slightly developed? Or was it a phenomenal exhibition of animal mind affected by an imperfect intellectual impulse; just as we see the electric currents sometimes checked, reversed, and perform a similar kind of act in their own domain of operation?

Or take the hypnotic. I put him into the mesmeric sleep and make him do several things and tell him that he is to forget them all when I awake him. I then have him use the coins in his mouth as I have described, and I tell him he must remember that. Now I awaken him and he forgets all I told him to forget, but remembers about the coins. I put him to sleep again and fix my mind on a piece of sugar and tell him I am going to give him some sugar; it is sweet, and to eat it, and then hand him a piece of sour apple. He sees only sugar, and and eats it tasting only sugar. And so with whatever I fix his attention on. Then while asleep, I tell him he must remember about the coins when he wakes, and a week hence at four o'clock (or any other fixed time ahead), he must go to sleep, use the coins in the same way, wake up and forget all about it afterward. Then I waken him. He remembers. At the time fixed he will become hypnotized, use the coins, wake up, and forget all about it. Here my mind force makes impression on him through the senses and he has no mind but mine. He hears me, and whatever I say is real to him, though it has no real existence in fact. If I give him a button and say it is a peach, he will see a peach. The activity and sensibility of any part of him will be suspended if I say it is suspended. I tell him he cannot feel in his cheek, and I may run a knife in it and he will feel nothing. He will hear a piano in a whistle if I tell him it is so, and he cannot hear at all if I say so. He thinks with me and has no will but my will, but that will must be expressed to him. Whatever I suggest is active, and no more, like the acting thought in the sleep-walker. Meantime, the animal functions go on undisturbed. The impressions made on him through the ear, produce in him the thought I suggest, and he has no other thought except those in harmony with that thought. There is no change of temperature in fact; but to him it is cold or hot, as I suggest it to him. Are there conductors that transfer to him my own mind force, and does the current continue in circuit as long as the hypnotic condition remains? Is there a combination of the animal and intellectual mind energies of both that in some way produces a modified force that operates to suspend his mind force, only so far as it can receive impressions and impulse through my mind energy?

Let us look at a cataleptic a moment. The instances are innumerable where, while in the cataleptic sleep, he has told of things that were going on at the time miles away—within the circle of his acquaintance—seeing it plainly as if present and looking at it with his eyes. Was there a conductor of some kind, by which the mind force passed and repassed and impressions were made from a distance, as the electric current started here makes an impression miles away?

I am in a strange city. Suddenly I think of some one I have not thought of or seen for years, and do not know that he is living. I turn a corner, or within a few steps, meet that person. Had mind force found a conductor and found its way between us and made an impression?

I am sitting in my room, and suddenly the house of a relative an hundred miles away comes before me and some one seems to say to me, "Come at once. Your brother is dead." I am so impressed that I cannot throw it off, and I see the family in their sorrow. Soon after, a telegram brings me the same message. How was it; had conditions of body, mind and exterior electric and magnetic forces, or in some other way, created such conditions that mind force there had come to me and impressed me here? Similar incidents are of daily occurrence, and in some form at some time have come into the life of most persons. The instances of thought transference have been too numerous to permit of successful contradiction.

The control of the mind over the body is almost unlimited. The strong mind controls the weak one. There may be great mental force in a feeble body, as in the case of the late Alexander H. Stephens; and a weak mind in a giant's body.

The mind is just what impressions made through the bodily senses have created. These impressions depended entirely on the character of the sensorium that received them, and the environments of the individual when made. The criminal's mind could not be other than it is, with his physical organism and environments during the formation of mind force up to the time of offense. The impressions made on his sensorium and the impulses created by those impressions, have been the ruling force, have given him the mind force he has, and it can act only within the circuit that will furnish conductors for its impulses.

Let us look at the intermingling of mind forces between different persons. We see instances all about us. Two persons—perfect strangers—meet, and with no knowledge of each other, without speaking, with no apparent cause, they are mutually repulsive to each other, or mutually attractive; or one may repel and the other attract. If these persons continue to meet, those who repel at first may attract afterwards; or the reverse. Some may grow more repulsive as time passes. Yet there is no outward offensiveness or other apparent reason. Are there conductors, and is there an actual meeting of the mind energies, evolving new or modified forces, as in the meeting of the ends of the magnetic needles? With some persons, when the mind forces meet, there seems to be a mingling of the energies, without any special attraction, affinity or disturbance, and so continues. This occurs in ordinary sociability, and forms sets or circles in social life. In some cases there is mild attraction, harmonious mingling, and no actual affinity. Such are ordinary friendships; a step beyond the merely social. Sometimes there is strong attraction at one time with apparent, but no real affinity, and then strong repulsion and disturbance, but still a mingling of mind forces. Such persons are alternately quarreling and making up—great friends at one time, and enemies at another, and so alternating. Sometimes there is strong attraction, close commingling, some affinity, but no union. It is often mistaken for love, and marriages are founded on it. In reality, it is only admiration—an emotion easily destroyed. If such persons are kept constantly together, as in marriage, they become sensitive, are easily shocked and repelled at times and attracted at others. There is mingling at all times and partial affinity on occasions only. With some persons there is partial affinity of part, partial union of part, and repulsion of other parts. In such case they are persons who cannot stay together without discord, or remain apart without misery, and they are alternately separating and uniting; always with a constant longing when apart to be together, and always feeling some shock or repugnance

when together. With some there is partial affinity, easy commingling, and no repulsion ; and such persons are quiet and
peaceable when together and content when separated. There
is no strong attraction and no repulsion. We see instances in
the easy going-couples we sometimes meet, partners, or husband and wife; who never seriously differ, nor do they have
any demonstrations of affection ; no effusiveness when together and no worrying when separated. With yet others there
is gradual attraction—in rare cases sudden and violent attraction—commingling, affinity, and actual union of the mind energies. In most cases it is slow and graded, depending on
knowledge as it is developed through successive impressions,
ending in final union and cohesion of the two energies. This
is what may be called love, and the only true love—a thing of
growth, where each is the other and both are each. It is natural marriage. But few formal marriages are founded on it. In
reality it is marriage itself, and the legal or clerical ceremony
of marriage in such cases is only a necessary deference to the
law, on the grounds of public policy, but it adds nothing to
the indissoluble union that nature has made. In such marriages only can the true home be found ; such a home as
criminals never know. The influences from such a home they
never feel, nor can they be made to comprehend them. In
these illustrations we can see the impression one person makes
on the sensorium of another, with the thought impulse that
follows, and the harmonies or repulsions that attend them. ◦
Just how the subtile forces act, we cannot know, any more
than we can know why a beautiful and fragrant flower attracts
while another one may offend ; or why what attracts one will
offend another, and what offends one will attract another. It
is the thought impulse that follows the impression made on
each sensorium, which is peculiar to itself and like no other.

While we are soaring into the imaginary regions of the supernatural, to search for " spirit," and regarding this mind
force as a spiritual soul, and approaching the convict to impress something on this soul, we are looking far above the plane
on which that mind is moving ; entirely outside of its manner
of creation and action, the means by which it receives and re-
sponds to impressions, and so overlook and go wide of the

ways that alone can lead us to gain the most practical access to it. If we will cease to live in an imaginary realm, and come back to our own plane; if we will regard this mind as what it is—a substantial, material force, inherent in, and born of matter, and having no tangible existence elsewhere so long as the body in which it is generated and acts is vital; instead of trying to regard it as an immaterial force of supernatural origin, and capable of being impressed by other than natural forces, if we will take cognizance of how it starts, note how it grows, what makes it and how it can be enlarged or its power diminished, we shall be better able to impress it as we would like to have it impressed, and thus produce responsive impulses in the direction of higher thoughts and more moral influences. The open way to the celestial plane can be reached only through some conception of the sublime perfection and wisdom embodied in matter and the operation of natural material forces,

Many things in connection with mental force are, as yet, inexplicable. Instances are common of persons who are kindly, good-natured, moral, and of general good disposition when sober, but who when drunk are demons of cruelty and destructiveness. As if in the ganglions of combativeness and destructiveness there lurks a latent, undeveloped condition or property, which is temporarily developed by the stimulus of alcohol on the animal mind, while at the same time the counteracting ganglia become stupefied and subdued and fail to generate any moral force. In other words, the impressions made on the sensorium through the senses create impulses in form of thoughts for torture and destruction, and none for the opposite of these. On the other hand, there are morose, ugly, vicious, quarrelsome persons when sober, who become good-natured, humorous, and affectionate when drunk. In each case the impressions on the sensorium and the impulses generated by them, are entirely different when sober from what they are when drunk; and it would indicate an abnormal or diseased condition of the tables on which the impressions are made. It is much like a sensitized plate on which to impress a picture with the camera, together with the arrangement of the light and adjustment of the camera, corresponding to the tables of the

brain, the nerves, the physiological and pathological conditions
of the body. Every imperfection or want of proper adjustment, will affect the impression, as in an electric manifestation
where electricity is spread over a metallic surface, if there be
rusted spots on the metal and the current be strong, at those
spots it will be obstructed, will accumulate, and to a greater
or less degree heat, or destroy the metal and consume the
rusted particles. So in the ganglions, there may be imperfect
development or formation, or material, which are not affected
by the ordinary physical energy; but when it is stimulated by
alcohol, the circulation increased and the vital force made
more vigorous, these usually latent places are acted on in such
manner as to produce the impulses manifested. These facts
are of grave importance when we come to inflict punishment
on convicts. We are making impressions through the senses
to create mind force, and what latent elements we may arouse
by the stimulus is of consequence. It may be a question
whether persons affected as I have stated, are morally responsible when excited, further than for using alcohol knowing its
effects. It is not unlike manifestations among the insane, and
the phases it assumes are endless. A person usually amiable,
when they become offended may become morose and pout for
months. Some never overlook an offense. Others not usually
amiable, may grow momentarily savage on offense, but quickly
recover and become pleasant. One may see a bright side to
everything and laugh at calamity, another may see no sun-
shine in anything and brood in melancholy continually. Yet
each and all are the immediate results of impressions made on
the sensorium through the nerves by the action in matter outside of and in the body; as is also, the results of the compound and complicated action of accumulated remembered
thought from continuous impressions; and the thoughts they
develop constitute what we call mind, or the visible manifestations of mental force, in its turn acting wholly through matter. In a word, we can have no conception of what is not
material.   .

I said that mind is not confined to what we call intellect and
our own consciousness. Matter has mind and conscious intelligence, and though it may extend to but one impression and one

act, it is intelligent as to its proper affinity, position and office, and cannot be made to take any other position or perform any other office than the one belonging to it and which it intelligently recognizes always.   The particles of matter to make a hair; to provide the gland, the nerve, the blood vessel, the oil sac, the capillary substance; to shape the hair into a tube and provide and distribute the coloring matter, make no mistakes.   Each intelligently selects its own material, rejects all else, performs the physiological, chemical, mechanical manipulations required, and in such harmony with each other as to intelligently accomplish the purpose, The sensorium takes no cognizance of it except in the visible results.   There is the still more mysterious exhibition of energy and force which I have called the physiological or animal mind, in the involuntary muscles; where there is no intellectual mind yet so intimately connected with it that the former can be visibly and vitally affected by the latter; but the animal mind can go on intelligently and perfectly without the intellectual; as in sleep, coma, in the infant, the utter idiot, and cases of total insensibility, in paralysis, etc.   The processes of circulation, digestion, nutrition, and waste go on. The hydraulic and rhythmic action of the heart and the breathing are uninterrupted.   Each part performs its office intelligently.   And it would do so if the intellectual brain were removed, the residue being uninjured, under the stimulus of electricity, as I have shown in the chapter on mentality.   What is the energy that compels it and regulates it?   Like other energies it is a property in, of, with and by matter, and non-existent without it.   This animal mind goes on the same, modified at times by intellectual mind force when that is intelligently active, but independent of mind or no mind, other than its own, as a whole.   It is perpetual motion until the matter is exhausted—worn out—that creates the energy; or until violence breaks the current, as in the case of electricity.   When intellectual mind is absent it consciously and intelligently performs the functions belonging to it, as the current on the telegraph continues to flow, though the key of the register may be turned off and repeat no message.   And a continuous inflow of force from action in matter external to and in the body, returns through visible manifestations by the

body, in part as completely mechanical as the workings of a
steam engine under the mysterious force of the invisible steam
converted from water in the boiler, by the mysterious combus-
tion of matter in the furnace, kept in operation by the human
mechanism, which is driven by mind force, generated in the
sensorium, fed by physiological operation of nutrition derived
from food. Mind converted into fire and steam, and that
again by machinery into something to use, making more impressions—more mind.

The words energy and force convey an idea, but they do not
explain. Mind is force, energy, anything we may please to
call it that conveys an idea of power, subtle, invisible, mysterious, known only through visible results of its action on matter. Is this energy atomic? Are electricity, ether, magnetic
force, and all other agencies? Their forms and combinations
change and are infinite in modes of manifestation, and they
are found only in connection with what is atomic. Can we conceive of anything not so, though we may not be able to weigh,
measure or analyze it? The temporary forms of their combinations alone are destructible, and we may justly believe they
are themselves eternal.

There was a time when this energy now converted into conscious intelligent mind force did not exist in that form. It is
not illogical to believe that it is deathless, and that when the
physical environment in which it is developed here shall lose
its vitality, it may continue to exist on some other plane, in
some other form, and that communication between that plane
and this one be possible. Where or what that or those planes
is or are is beyond us, but that they exist and that we can, in
some degree, penetrate them, has received many apparant
demonstrations, and is being evidenced to some extent by the
most careful scientific investigation by the ablest philosophical
inquirers in the world. We rest content with referring to it as
psychic and telepathic force, for want of better knowledge. It
may be the operation of mind on planes provided for it by the
Supreme Architect, which planes are intercommunicable to
some extent, now to us unknown, but the extent of which is
dependent upon conditions of various character. I have no
reference to ordinary spirit manifestations, but to those that

come within the domain of scientific investigations, as given
to us from time to time by the best minds of the age. If it be
a delusion it is a comforting one, and we shall never know it
as such.

Regarding mind as I do other subtle and invisible forces—as
material—I find a satisfactory solution of many things otherwise mysterious, and in this view there is nothing antagonistic
to a rational theology, to religion, to belief in a future existence for this intelligent force in form for intelligent action, on
a higher or lower plane; while it frees me from useless effort
in trying to comprehend spirit, which is an impossibility,
leading to confusion and unreason. I can account ration-
ally for many things relating to persons found in the crime
class that are otherwise incomprehensible. This mind is the
thing we approach and have to deal with when the convict
comes under our care in the prison. In him it is an unbalanced force, operating inharmoniously, and it is the material
force created and maintained by the impressions that have
been made through the senses and the impulses those impressions have produced. The character of those made and to be
made, did and must depend entirely on the character of the
physical matter that receives them, and the kind of impulse—
thought—following, and the operations of that impulse (combined with all others in action) in acts, depend upon the
change that matter undergoes in producing the impulse, and
in manifesting itself. The effort to be made with him is, to
restore or create a balance, and harmonious action. Create
such physical conditions that the impressions made will generate impulses and thoughts tending to moral, rational, practical
acts, harmonious with the best desires, objects and ends in life.
If I go groping in the dark, feeling for a ghost, trying to drag
it to the light, to find I can neither see or comprehend it because it is immaterial, though I can feel that I have got it, I
am at such disadvantage contending with a paradox as to render my labor useless. But if I know the mind is a material
force dependent on physiological conditions of the body with
its peculiar supply and waste, the impressions that have been
made on it by environment, with such knowledge of its origin
in each individual as is obtainable; what changes must be

made by creating other conditions that will receive different impressions and generate different impulses, I am not only better able to judge if such change can be made, but what methods can and should be used to effect it. When I come to study the criminal and experiment with him with a view to reformation, I am dealing with something material that I can comprehend, and not with something immaterial of which I can have no comprehension.

That peculiar element now being studied in connection with mind phenomena, called hypnotism or hypnosis, to which I have alluded, comes before us as something almost appaling, when we recognize the power of the strong mind over the weak one. The now indisputable fact that the hypnotic can be made to remember or forget as he is directed to do, after being awakened, and that he can be directed to do something at some time in the future and then forget it, and he will do it and forget it, a new world of mystery and danger opens before us. How much of this element that can be so acted on by other minds, has peculiar properties that act on itself, that make people lose and forget themselves, to find themselves far from home and in situations they are unfitted for and at war with their whole previous life, with no memory of what they have done? How many mysterious crimes are committed by hypnotics under self-imposed sleep or that imposed by others, of which the perpetrator knows nothing? How many having the power use subjects for criminal purposes, the subjects themselves being helpless and having no memory of it afterward? How completely morality and virtue is defenseless in the one who can be operated on, if in the presence of one who can influence them, with the opportunity and the will to do so? The history of strange things, that are to us incredulous and regarded as degrading superstitions, are less strange than some of the developments of modern investigation. And few present more incredible features than are coming to light under the exercise of this hypnotic influence. Already it has been suggested to make it a crime to practice hypnotism, or give any public exhibitions of it. There can be little doubt that hypnosis, catalepsy, somnambulism, epilepsy, hysteria, insanity and other mysterious mental manifestations are outgrowths of an allied nature from peculiar physical conditions, creating or permitting of peculiar mental organization. There is something in the brain and nerve texture that permits of impressions in some persons by electric, magnetic, 'or some un-known force, and of the evolution and application of the force to make those impressions in some other persons, that cause these manifestations. The origin and operation of the force calls for serious consideration in the study of the prison ques-tion.

CHAPTER VI.

TURNING to the proposition that all progress is in reaction—the maintenance of equilibrium, that nothing is
lost in action and reaction in matter—it is proper to consider
briefly some of the operations of and results from natural
forces. Nature demands and will have compensation for all
she gives us. She always makes even and exact payment.
She gives away nothing. Whether we receive blessing or
curse we earn it first, or it has been earned for us. There is
no charity in her disposition. Whatever we desire to do, or
attempt to do, this should be constantly borne in mind, for we
cannot change her inexorable decrees in the least particular.

Whatever happens to us is a natural outgrowth from the
action of natural forces, and is a direct consequence of our
mentality and environment. The mind force, or energy, of
every person is the outgrowth of physical formation and subsequent environment; the surroundings and nurture day by
day make up the education and fix the mental impressions,
and the plane on which each person acts, and whatever happens to them on that plane is the result of the operation of
natural forces on that plane; that is to say, whatever happens
to the person is the result of his mental organism, as originally
formed and progressively developed and educated, constituting
his mentality, and is the exact response of natural laws.

Take a very extreme case for illustration. I am on the
street going home from my business. No matter if that business be begging, or banking, or stealing, or what not. One
person shoots at another, misses, and kills me. It is a natural
result and the immediate natural compensation of my own
acts, acts dictated by my own mentality and with my surroundings as they had been and were, on the plane where I was then
acting. So also, of the one who did the shooting and of the

one he designed to kill. My mentality and environment from birth to that time had brought into operation natural forces in such order of sequence as to place me exactly in the position to receive that bullet at that time. Had I started a little sooner or later, walked a little faster or slower, lived in some other direction, been in some other business, or in a different state of health, I would not have been in that spot. The subjects of right and wrong, of accident and design, do not enter into the matter at all and are wholly foreign to it, so far as I am concerned. If they have any connection with it they relate to the shooter and his intended victim. But had their mentality and environment through life been different, they would not have been there. The result of the operation of natural forces are never accidental. We use the word "accident" as we do others, for comparison. Had one single ganglion of my brain at birth been differently organized or in different combination in my organism, my environment in some respects would have been different. The impulses created would have made my acts different and my place at the time of shooting would have been elsewhere, as a result of natural forces operating under the different conditions following the different mentality and environment.

There is no possible chance to argue on a matter of fact, while we may on a matter of opinion. That the energies and forces of nature so operate with the individual as to make exact compensation in all cases is a fact; that is, he receives exactly what his own acts have led him to, regardless of design, and as a result of the action of natural forces with existing conditions. A man can act no further than he can perceive. To enlarge the boundaries of his perceptions in one or more directions, without maintaining mental balance, may benefit or may injure him, and others through him, as he may possess or lack the ability to act judiciously within the enlarged boundaries. Take a feeble-minded person—child or adult—with a mental organism that tends to crime—say arson, larceny or murder—and give it knowledge by teaching, enlarging its boundary of perception. Unless you also give it moral perception, and moral will to dominate those tendencies, the increased knowledge will be used for vicious purposes.

Nature acts as in other cases in making compensation. So with convicts in prison. Making them wiser and giving them skill in labor while under restraint, makes them the more dangerous to society when liberated, unless the moral balance is also educated so it performs the office of holding the evil impulses in restraint.

We may aptly refer again to the boiler and engine and attached machinery. We have the steam and machinery, but lack the proper regulating, governing and adjusting provisions to make them work properly. To provide this, we increase the capacity of the working machinery and add to the quantity of steam, with no adequate adjustment of the regulating machinery. The consequences that must follow are evident. So with the convict. We add to his physical strength by discipline, labor and regularity of habits; to his intellectual powers by teaching; but, unless we can also elevate and perfect his moral perceptions so they can regulate both the animal and intellectual forces we have increased, he will be injured instead of benefitted, and will be more able to injure others if set at large. The views of prison wardens, directors, managers, chaplains and legislative committees, are as variant on these subjects as is their personality and intelligence, and with an occasional exception, the matter has never been considered by them from a scientific point of view. Whether from want of knowledge, or because of belief in other theories or supposed theories, makes no difference. The fact remains that it has not generally been philosophically considered. This fact is true, also, of a majority of the philanthropists and reformers who are seeking by various means to benefit the unbalanced portion of humanity.

One man stands on a high building and looks at the street below. Another stands on the ground at the bottom and looks at the same street. They cannot see it alike nor can they act alike in relation to it. Let them change places, and still they will not see it exactly alike, nor can they act alike in relation to it in everything, unless their preceptions be exactly alike, and that is not possible. They may act on a general line in harmony and accomplish a purpose, but there will be mental differences in views.

Out of this universal difference comes the progressive energies that make what we call civilization; but the equilibrium of good and evil has been maintained, being changed only in forms and operations, and place of manifestations.

If we can acquire, keep, and judiciously use knowledge, we shall get the most there is in life for us, and that to the extent we can become keepers and users. In these words, "the ability to acquire, keep, and judiciously use," to whatever applied, lies the entirety of philosophy and science, which is no more or less than truth demonstrated. While truths may be innumerable we can make practical use of only a portion of them in securing the best for ourselves through life, as individuals and in associations. That portion we must judiciously use or they become evils; truths operating as falsehoods; good producing evil; realities not real, having only the appearance.

So with money and property. If we can acquire, keep and judiciously use, we can keep out of the reach of want and enjoy whatever of comforts they can confer. If we cannot, we must be and remain dependent on the will of those who can do so. Judicious use includes practical moral perception, with the will to use it as a controlling force. This carries us back to the foundation—the mentality and environment, and the natural forces set and kept in operation by them. Illustrations are before us constantly. Some time ago a millionaire in one of our large cities forced "a corner" (secured control of) on a leading staple in food supplies. To that time he had possessed the faculties that enabled him to acquire, keep and judiciously use knowledge and money and property. In forcing this "corner" he laid aside his moral balance and used his knowledge and money injudiciously. The "corner" was broken and left him a bankrupt. Returning to a judicious use again, he is once more a millionaire.

There is Jones. His hands are about the size of those of a well-grown girl of twelve years and as soft a baby's. They have worked only in kid gloves. He is a silk weaver and knows nothing else. He has worked at it all his life and grew up in a silk mill. He has a wife and five children. His wages have barely supported them, but his abilities have not enabled him to acquire and keep anything, and his perceptions have not enabled him to adapt his burdens and responsibilities to his means. He has both knowledge and skill in his trade but has not the faculty to judiciously use either in adapting himself to his environment. The mill is burned, or there is a strike, or the firm fails, or the works are shut down in a panic. Jones is out of work and he can do nothing but weave silk. His mental organization and environment have placed him right there, and starvation stares him right in the face unless he seeks relief from the poor rates. Take what case you will and the same answer must be returned. The conditions are the results of natural forces and they are irresistible. As far as we can learn their operations we can adapt our actions; but we cannot change them to meet our impulses.

In order to turn a day laborer, who cannot get beyond his plane and environment as such, into a capitalist and employer, he must be born again, thus: if his perceptions and ability to act can be changed, by education in any form, so that he can "acquire, keep, and judiciously use," he can begin to progress toward the position he would have occupied, had his original mental organization and environment given him those faculties. The questions of right and wrong as between rich and poor have nothing to do with it. The only questions are such as relate to existing conditions and the most practical ways of dealing with those conditions. The conditions are hard facts and sentimentalities are out of place in the processes of reasoning by which a practical way is sought.

A Jay Gould may acquire, keep and use a hundred millions of dollars. A John Johnson may not be able to secure enough to eat, and he has a wife and several children. How can the conditions be changed so as to give the Goulds less and the Johnsons more? One class of speculators say, " by legal enactments." Another says, "by moral and religious instructions and prayer for Divine aid." Still another says, " by socialistic organization, and anti-poverty associations." Last, comes the " Nationalist," and says, " Let government carry on all business, mobilize the people as employés, control and furnish and manage everything." Well, all may be made factors in a movement, but neither will accomplish the improvement desired. Johnson must be given such instructions as will give him the faculties to "acquire and keep, and judiciously use."

Now, the question is placed between us and the natural forces. Johnson is as he is; his mentality and environment must be taken as they are. Has he the mental organism that will enable him to acquire the education, enlarge his perceptions, so he can acquire, or acquire and keep, or acquire, keep and use? He may be taught to acquire, but not to keep; or to acquire and keep, but not to use; or to acquire and use, but not judiciously. If he has not the faculty to acquire all, he cannot be advanced. Legislation could not do it; for if you could say by law that Gould shall have only ten thousand dollars— or any other sum—and if he gets any more he shall divide with Johnson, no matter by what process, it could not be enforced. And if it could be, Johnson could not keep and judiciously use it and would waste it. If his tendencies are immoral he would use it viciously. So it all comes back to the proposition, that all who can acquire, keep and judiciously use opportunities or means in a practical way, will dominate and govern those who cannot do so, and they will frame and conduct government for themselves. to which the others must submit.

Under that government new questions will constanly arise and must be dealt with as they come and grow, each giving rise to others. As to all of them, natural forces will work out their legitimate ends. If obstructed in one direction they will form new combinations and operate in other directions, bringing exact compensation in all cases. The amelioration of the condition of the defective and unfortunate classes and the curbing of the unhealthy ambition of others, is action worthy of all those of good intellect and moral tendencies, and is a necessity to a true civilization. But when we ask, "How shall it be done?" we must lay aside all sentimentality, take conditions just as they exist, recognize the natural forces, seek for practical methods adapted to the mental calibre and condition of those to be affected, and right here is the point of departure between practical truth and sentimentality.

Charitable and prison associations, and all other reformers, must practically recognize the facts here stated before they can make permanently beneficial progress in effecting reforms. The conditions demand a system of education and training through some generations of teaching, tending to knowledge that will aid in the pro-creation of better mentality, in place of the offspring from indiscriminate indulgence within or without the marriage relations, which law and custom now permits, and largely sanctions, too many of which are deformed, diseased, or deficient in mind and body. And this is a first requisite to permanent reform.

The infinite laws governing matter—animate and inanimate —come into existence with it. Mankind as a part of animate matter forms no exception. Deity acts only through those laws, and we know them as natural forces so far as we have knowledge. Any special interposition by him to obstruct them would destroy equilibrium and chaos would come. Ignorance in relation to those laws by individuals hinders each in securing the best for themselves, separately and in the aggregate. Even where they are known there is more or less disregard of them, or efforts to thwart their operation, and then, to cure evils that follow the efforts by further obstruction.

In every relation in life we seek to destroy that which is dangerous and vicious, except with ourselves as animals. In this instance we seem to do our best to produce and perpetuate that which is most vicious and dangerous, by reckless gratifications of mere animal impulses in many directions. When the natural forces bring the exact compensation, we strive to reject it and secure some other, by expedients which those forces will not allow of adaptation to such ends. This method of evasion, and trying to substitute some artificial in place of natural force, is the line on which too many reformers waste their labor, while they produce antagonisms that create class prejudice, and want of confidence in all reformers, on the part of those who are sought to be benefitted.

It has been objected that this view of natural force is fatality. Not at all, as fatality is understood. The theologian will learn from the inspired source of his philosophy that "the leopard cannot change his spots," and that "as a man thinketh so is he." Quotations can be multiplied. Had the leopard been born a tiger he would have no spots, and he must act on

the plane he is fitted for. So the thoughts the man thinketh
and that make him what he is, are like the leopard's spots and
he cannot change them unless his mentality can be changed.
That may be done in some cases and in others it cannot, by
change of environment and the development of mental force
now latent and inactive, or creating it if non-existent. So can
the leopard's spots be changed by domestication and chemical
washes, and in either case new forces spring into activity under
the new environment, and whatever happens on the new plane
is the legitimate result of natural forces, produced still by the
mentality and surroundings of the individual. Fatality is a
fixed condition, in which there can be no change and from
which there can be no escape. The mentality of the child
born in the slums, with the surroundings of the slums, will fix
its plane, and all that happens on it will be the direct result of
its mentality and environment, and if left there its fate is fixed.
It can never rise above the level of that plane. But it is not
fatality, for his surroundings and mentality may be changed,
and on the new plane so made for it, its fate will be different.
Fatality knows no change. Hence the view presented is not
fatality. The same facts apply to the convict in prison, but
with less ability to effect change. His mental organs are less
impressible than the child's. His experience involves a larger
memory of evil surroundings; evil impressions are more hardened and crystallized; it is more difficult to secure favorable
surroundings and more difficult to adapt him to them than in
the case of the child. Yet in many cases it is possible, and
a higher plane may be reached.

CHAPTER VII.

MARRIAGE.

THE three important events in every life are birth, marriage and death. On birth depends the physical and mental organism, and that again depends on marriage. The physical and mental status of succeeding generations depends on marriage in the preceding generations. Over his birth man has no control. Over his death he has partial control, for by wise use of the knowledge within his reach he can prolong his lease of life. Over his marriage he has entire control. Marriage is the most important event connected with human life. Its importance cannot be overrated. Yet, it receives less serious and practical consideration than any other thing. Marriage is generally regarded as something within the domain of romance, mixed up more or less with love and passion; sometimes including the mercenary among the incidents, and sometimes the compulsory, without love. The Church regards it as a sacrament—a holy covenant; and the state declares it a civil contract, into which females from sixteen to eighteen years of age may enter, while they are not qualified to enter into any other contract under twenty-one years.

In fact, marriage is the very highest and most serious order of business; and there is no action in his life in which man should use every element of judgment with such scrupulous care as in contracting marriage. Usually, marriage is supposed to be founded on love. In truth, love is the outgrowth of marriage. Love is usually regarded as a passion, but it is not. Passion is impulsive, short-lived, and soon consumes itself. Love is of slow growth, and will germinate and flourish only in the soil of profound respect; respect born of knowledge that its object is worthy of it, and it appeals to the highest intelligence and purest motives. It cannot be founded on temporary impressions, however favorable. Admiration is mistaken

71

for profound respect and for love. The impulses following,
may stimulate the imagination to clothe the object with the
most lovable qualities, feed passion with dreams and reveries
full of romance, but it is not love. Marriage under such a
supposition leaves the parties to awaken sooner or later to a
feeling of restraint, and they long to, if they do not break
through it. All the caution, inquiry, investigation and thorough
continued effort one is capable of making, should be brought
into operation to ascertain if the conditions exist to create
mutual and profound respect. Unless they do, there can never
be any real love. If they do, love will grow there and be strong
and vigorous; growing stronger as time passes; enduring;
never wearying; like the ivy and the oak, inseparable even in
death. In this, as in other cases, what we call accident, but
really the outgrowths of conditions — sometimes forms unions
on real love without this investigation, but it is seldom.
Hence so much domestic discord.

The man and woman who so marry will not rear criminals,
or scrofulitics, or idiots. They will not be parties to the procreation of deformities, disease and criminal mentalities. As I
have shown in the chapter on " Mind," marriage is the absolute *union* of two minds. Not the temporary attraction and
mingling of two mind energies, but the actual union of those
energies, so blended and united that each lives in the other
and for the other, and each seeks to keep itself worthy to be
respected and loved by a common impulse.

This, and this alone, is true marriage. Neither church or
state can add to or take from it. Public policy requires certain formalities called marriage and the law authorizes certain
persons to perform them, but that is only the evidence of the
civil contract. With the mind union there is the real marriage.
Without the mind union it is only a contract. In any case the
legal contract operates only to secure certain private and public legal rights.

The legitimate objects of marriage are to establish and maintain an orderly and moral relation between the sexes, and
make provisions for the proper nurture and protection of the
offspring that may follow that relation. To prevent promiscuous commerce between the sexes and the debasing conse-

quences attendant. To create home circles, close domestic
relations, and the foundation for social conditions that are elevating in influence, and admit of limited action for the preservation of morality and liberty.

The state has taken charge of the subject of marriage and
undertakes to regulate it by statute; declares it a civil contract
between a man and a woman; how it may be made and how
annulled; what the personal and property relations as between
the parties, and the personal and legal obligations as to each
other, their offspring, society and the state shall be, during life,
at separation, and in case of death. It allows only one existing contract and authorizes judicial officers and ministers of the
church to perform the ceremony. It requires a state's license
to be taken out, fixes the conditions for license, levies a tax for
its issue, requires a record to be kept of the license and the cer-
tificate of the officer as to the ceremony under it. In certain
cases of minority it requires sworn statements as to age, and
consent of parent or guardian. It prohibits marriage between
certain persons, declares marriage void in certain cases, and exercises complete control and jurisdiction over the persons and
subject-matter at the will of the legislature, as it deems best
for the public policy, regardless of any of the real or supposed
rights or liberties of the person as an individual. But it
reaches a most "lame and impotent conclusion" in its provisions and there stops, leaving the doors wide open to the entrance of irreparable evils, and by its provisions as made, and
its omissions to make other provisions, it invites the entrance
of those evils, and sanctions and protects their authors when
they come. That is to say, it creates conditions out of which
natural forces irresistibly produce those evils in their legitimate
operations.

Here begins the dividing line between wisdom and unwis-
dom in the law. Here lies the utter inconsistency in the
motive of the legislature regulating marriage with a view to
protecting individuals and the public; a pretence of affording
protection and at the same time not infringe the "liberty of
the citizen." In regulating marriage the law says that none
shall marry within the third degree of consanguinity, and in
some states the fourth, because marriage between near blood

relations is likely to produce offspring deformed or diseased, physically and mentally. Insane and idiots shall not marry, because they cannot make a contract and because of hereditary tendency to produce idiots and insanity. It makes it a crime to marry in any of these cases. In this, it aims to prevent degenerate offspring and protect individuals and society against the evils that would attend such offspring.

But, if the vilest mortal that can live—one not in these classes—sees proper to marry, the law issues the license for the asking, takes the fee, makes the record, and leaves the offspring and society to shift for themselves in the best way they can. The confirmed inebriate, the weak-minded and semi-idiotic, the confirmed criminal, the offspring of the half-witted and insane, if lucid at the time, the incurably diseased, the scrofulitic, the syphilitic, the hereditary pauper, the depraved and reckless—even paupers while in the poorhouse and criminals while in jail are in every way encouraged, given license, and are protected by the law. No thought is taken for the unfortunate offspring, or for the body politic or social, and the irreparable evils that must fall upon all. The church adds its sanction and its ministers aid in making these civil contracts, by performing the ceremony with prayers and benedictions. Not in all cases, but in too many. If it is wise to prohibit polygamy, marriage between near relations, between the insane and idiotic, because of heredity and transmission of evils, it is equally wise to prohibit it in all cases where like evils may follow. If the law has the power to prohibit and punish violation in the one case, it has equal right in all others.

There is an endless procession of children from all these sources coming into the mass of the population to live lives of crime, immorality, want, suffering, misfortune, and degeneration, transmitting the taint in constantly widening streams, generation after generation, with the ultimate certainty of the deterioration of the race, and final irreparable degeneracy. With the utmost care for prevention, there will be enough diseased and deformed from accident and violations of law to tax the energies of the people in preserving morals, and intellectual supremacy and progress. But with this constant tide, bearing the scum of reprobacy and vice, ebbing and flowing through the social sea and depositing its baneful sediment and froth everywhere, on every shore, there can be but one final end. It is simply appalling to recognize it, much more to reflect upon it.

The reason given for the absence of legislative prohibition is, that it would be an infringement "upon the liberty of the citizen;" the rights of the individual; and that the prohibitory legislation could not be enforced. Let us see how far this position is tenable.

A man wants to run a steamer to carry passengers and freight. The law disregards his individual rights. It says, "You can't do it. But if you will have your boat examined by government officials and she is admitted to registry, and you are found qualified to navigate her, license will be given to you. The lives and property of others must be protected." So if one wants to act as pilot, to bring vessels out and into the harbor, or run a tug for towing them; both must submit to examination and be found fit for the position. The safety and welfare of the public is alone considered. A man wants to retail liquors. The law says, "You cannot do it only on specific conditions. Petition the county court or board, and get a certain number of responsible freeholders and householders to join you. Set forth the exact lot and room where you are to sell. Give notice publicly in a paper and by posting when and where the petition will be heard, so others can appear and oppose it if they desire. Go before the court, prove your notice, prove the qualifications of your co-petitioners, prove by reliable evidence that you are a man of good moral character, fit to be trusted with a license and that you do not get drunk yourself. Contract with the state that you will not sell on election days or on any public holidays, nor to minors, nor persons intoxicated, nor in the habit of becoming so; nor sell on Sundays, or before five A. M., nor after 10 P. M.; that you will keep an orderly house, and pay to any person all damages they may sustain because of any violation of the contract on your part. Execute bond with security binding you to this contract. Then pay into the treasury the sum required, and license will be given to you to sell in that room, at that place, to be drank there and nowhere else. On these conditions only can you have it." Why all this? Simply for protection of individuals and the public against possible injury. A man wants to practice law, or medicine, or pharmacy, or act as notary, and he is barred unless he submits to examination and shows a fitness for the place and its duties. When that is done license issues and not before. The instances can be multiplied indefinitely, and in many cases—like the notary—it involves only dollars and cents. And this to prevent injuries to the individuals and the public that are possible and not at all certain. In most cases they are very remote. In no one case is there any thought or fear of " infringing the rights of the citizen."

Now, if to prevent possible and not certain evils, the law can interfere and does interfere, why may it not and should it not interfere to prevent certain and irreparable evils and injury; not only to individuals, but to the entirety of the bodies corporal, social and political; not only for the present, but for generations without limit? Why should it not say to one who proposes to assume the marriage relation and become the possible and probable parent of offspring and the head of a family: "You must be fit for the place and able to assume and discharge the obligations and duties it will entail. You must show that no injury will come to individuals or the public. You must swear in your application that you do not come within the prohibited classes; and show that you are fit to be trusted with the grave responsibility?"

Is it any more an infringement on personal right than it is in case of selling liquor? Are the evils resulting from marriage by one wholly unfit for the relations greater and more far-reaching, or are they less than those possible in the incipient stages of whiskey and beer? Is it of more consequence to establish a board of health to prevent the sale of diseased meat, or isolate a small-pox patient, or quarantine one with scarlet fever or yellow fever or cholera, than it is to prevent the production of scrofulitic, syphilitic, criminal, idiotic, and incurably deformed and diseased children, and pauper children by the million, generation after generation? Is it of more importance to examine a glandered horse or lumpy-jawed ox and order them killed, lest some other horses or oxen become affected, and have an official commission for the business, than it is that a vile, diseased and debauched criminal, or a demented person should submit to examination when they would assume a relation that may send down their vicious taint for generations, and that there should be a competent official commission to do the business? Is the law wise or justified that compels the former and ignores the latter, on any claim or pretense whatever? Are the duties and relations to the public of a notary or pilot of more importance than those of the parent of children and the head of a family? The objection is clearly not tenable for a moment. Society has a right to protect itself against any and all evils and to punish or isolate offenders against its decrees, and it has the power by legal enactment. No individual liberty or right is paramount to the general good. The law may fix as many or more conditions to marriage in its regulations as it has made, and as may be necessary to guard against any evils growing out of the relation in any case, just as it has fixed those already on the statute. It may prohibit marriage between any kinds of persons it may deem proper. It may provide for examination of applicants for license by a proper board of examiners, and it may affix penalties for violation of its provisions. It may provide for the removal and isolation of such as violate them. It may even proceed to the emasculation of such as are especially vicious and dangerous, or who continue to violate the law and produce offspring tainted with vicious disease, or otherwise deformed or demented, being among the prohibited class. It may make provisions dispensing with personal examination in such cases and on such conditions as may be named ; or requiring it in specific cases only, and provide penalties for violation of provisions as in other cases of offense, and leave the parties to risk detection and punishment, by marrying without examination in cases where it may be required.

Another objection is, that men and women will not be restrained and that such prohibition would produce indiscriminate sexual commerce, with increased instead of diminished evils. It does not follow at all. The law-making power is ample to afford protection on every side. It can regulate the social evil as well as it can any other evil. It cannot make people any more perfect than the Almighty has done, but it can limit and restrain to a certain extent in the preservation of order and morals, and as to the social evils with others, it can provide for, license and regulate women and houses as well as it can for liquor and houses. It can establish a board of inspection and health and require cleanliness and submission to authority as well as it can for diseased provisions, contagious diseases, and dangerous illuminants, oils, and explosives, the use of firearms, and against the improper use and spread of fire. It can require them to be kept orderly and prohibit indulgence elsewhere, as well as it can with saloons and the sale of drugs, narcotics and poisons and other dangerous compounds, and can limit the hours during which they may be kept open, as it does in other cases where that is deemed important. For people who will have liquor, and poisonous drugs, and other dangerous compounds, it already provides, and it can make like provisions in any other respect where evils affect or may affect the public. It can as rightly, and much more properly and wisely do it, than it can provide for a public market with its stalls, rules, inpection and police supervision and market master, compel dealers to occupy it, pay for license, and prohibit the transaction of market business anywhere else, under penalties and punishment. It can imprison and perpetually isolate all who continue to violate its prohibitions and put it beyond their power to repeat offences. It can limit as to numbers and as to times and occasions for frequenting, as well as it can for saloon and market days and hours. It already declares adultery and fornication, and seduction, and keeping a house of ill-fame, and frequenting one, and associating with lewd persons, crimes. It can provide for and regulate places where and conditions under which a board of health and police surveillance can keep these evils in constant check and reduce them to the minimum that it is possible under human regulations, and prevent indiscriminate commerce. The lack of this board of health and police surveillance, as part of a license system, is the reason former attempts to license the social evil have failed. It has never been tried anywhere with such boards as a fixed part of a license system.

It seems to me that there is a moral obliquity that affects the entire mass of political, social and religious leaders and teachers on the subject here being considered. When we analyze the views and action throughout, the glaring inconsistency and unreasonableness that seems to fill them has no parallel in any other matter seriously affecting individual and the public welfare. Among the first is a false modesty, that is shocked by any allusions to the most evident and debasing facts, that stare everybody in the face on all sides; that rub against everybody at every turn; that legislators, reformers and clergymen are contending with incessantly. While the powers of human invention are making exhaustive efforts to provide for the safety and betterment of humanity in all directions, all eyes seem closed or blinded to the avenues that admit the most serious dangers to it. They can see that the would-be pharmacist, physician and accoucheur finds his way barred until he can show that he is qualified to deal with dangerous compounds, and with human health and life. They can see that the man who would become a soldier and learn the art of war, learn how to kill and maim people and attack and destroy property in war, whether he be soldier or footpad, finds entrance to the ranks barred until a government official strips him, examines him as to bodily perfection and health, and next as to mental ability and moral perception to learn the manual of arms, the routine of discipline and service, obedience to regulations and orders, and subordination to superiors. If he is found competent he can gain admission for only five years, and during that time the government must contract to keep him. If the same kind of man, or any man, wants to enter the matrimonial ranks, the doors are wide open. To protect itself against a bad soldier, or one it may have to keep in prison or hospital, for only five years at most, government requires and exercises every precaution. But the recruit in the matrimonial ranks may serve for life, and his influence extend to future generations, and he may fill a hospital or prison with his offspring. Surely, to know that one is qualified to beget and care for human beings fit to live, is as important as to know how to kill them. But it is immodest to present this last view.

The church devotes its time and energies to prove that every human body possesses an immortal spiritual body, that

is liable to future torture unless it be made perfect in morals
and truth, and that must be done while it remains within its
mortal shell. It pleads and raves for prohibition of liquors and
tobacco, for forced observance of Sunday, for forced attend-
ance on schools, for recognition of God, Christ, and the Protestant religion in the civil constitutions, and for sundry other
restraints and commands with penalties, in order to save these
imperiled souls. Reformers go about the land devising ways
and means to educate, civilize, provide for and elevate, the
ignorant, the degraded, the poverty stricken that pervade
every plane of human action, and wander in and out among
the people everywhere. And yet these, with general society
added, hold up their hands before their faces in horror, if some
honest soul who has truth for a guide, calls to them to look,
and points them to the source of the evils they are battling
with and tells them they are responsible for it all, for the law
is only their united will in statutory phraseology. That it is
the result of their voluntary blindness and false conception of
civil, moral and religious duties. That they are seeking to
deal with evil conditions alone, instead of the causes of them,
and while trying to mitigate the evils in the results, are sup-
porting, increasing and enlarging the causes. That on every
other plane of action they recognize and deal with the causes;
but with men and women they ignore the causes and battle
with results alone. That they regard domestic brutes as of
more importance than they do human beings.

This same fallacy as to " individual liberty " existed in relation to the cattle only a little while ago, and there are a few
fossils who advocate it yet. Swine, sheep, horses and other
stock were permitted to run at large and intermingle at will.
The country was full of " scrubs." A proposition to shut them
up was met with a howl of indignation and derision. But they
have been shut up. Even in the few places where yet permitted to run at large, the males are prohibited, and it is made
criminal for the owner to permit it. The breeding of live stock
is encouraged; state, society and church, vie with each other in
that encouragement, and attend exhibitions of improved brutes
and are unsparing in approval, plaudits and commendation of
the splendid results that have attended the process of dealing

with causes instead of conditions. The "scrubs" have disappeared; and in their places have come strong, sightly, intelligent, useful and profitable animals, for every kind of use and station. Women and children gaze with admiration and applause upon the splendid males and females among the many distinct breeds of horses, jacks, cattle, swine, sheep, fowls, dogs, cats, rabbits, goats, and other animals. There is no false modesty about it. But let it be even suggested that the very same laws apply to human animals, and the very same practices in relation to them will produce like results, and the disgust manifested tells the would-be benefactor that he is classed among the vulgar.

What kind of a divine economy would that be considered, which recognizes a moral distinction between a real brute with four legs and one with two? That would encourage the breeding of brutal, mangy children, and condemn the breeding of mangy colts or cattle? That would destroy a glandered horse and approve the rearing of syphilitic and scrofulitic children? Who would recognize such a divinity, much less worship it and make it the foundation for a religion, and churches, and consecrated teachers, and sacraments, and prayers, and hymns of praise? Can a human economy of that character be any more tolerable than a divine one would be? Can a human legislature, or church, or society, justly or wisely create and maintain or tolerate distinctions that a divine economy would not? Such a conclusion would be not only unworthy of a sane human intellect, but is a degredation of human intelligence to the level of brute intelligence.

History tells us of one people among the Grecian provinces that recognized what I am contending for and what a false use of the benefits of civilization now persists in ignoring. Sparta regarded the human race within her borders as of more value than her animals, and she legislated for it and sought to improve it as we do our animals, and with the most pronounced success. She had no stream of demented, deformed, diseased and criminal human offspring of like parentage, pouring into her social channels. No one unfit, was permitted to become a parent; and a more chivalrous, stalwart and beautiful race has never inhabited the earth. Without Sparta there would have been no Athens. Yet they were no more so than the race would be now, if the law, society, and the church would discard its fallacious reasoning, abandon its false and mistaken policies, leave behind its romance and sentimentalisms, lay down its superstitions, recognize the economy of a real divinity, adapt themselves to the operation of the natural, irresistible forces hurled into existence with matter by that divinity and apparent to all who will look for them, and deal with the causes of degenerate humanity instead of with the results of that degeneracy only.

What wisdom is there in the policy, or what truth is there in the religion, or what real charity is there in the benevolence, or what stability is there in the reform, that builds and maintains institutions for the insane, the feeble-minded, the foundlings, the paupers, the incurably diseased, the incorrigible youths, the felons, and the petty offenders; the taxation of sound, honest, moral and industrious people, and the forced conversion of the products of their labor to the maintenance of these places by the hundreds, all over the land; and at the same time, the permission of usages and social conditions that keep them constantly filled with inmates, yearly increasing in numbers and in physical and mental deterioration? What blindness is it that makes a distinction between a brutal, vicious, conscienceless, diseased male, going at large up and down the land without restraint, indulging his brutal impulses, leaving his diseased and viciously tainted offspring for the public to care for, whether he goes on four legs or two, and makes himself heard by a brutal roar or by articulated speech? And that believes a Divine Providence makes a distinction, and gives one an immortal soul to be saved or lost and to the other none, *and for that reason* the one with two legs must be tolerated and left at large? He may just evade the hand of the criminal law, and yet he may taint every moral element, trample on every moral law, disregard social decency and order, debauch virtue, make a bauble of chastity, defy and sneer at public opinion, furnish inmates for prisons, homes for abandoned women and children, lying-in hospitals, paupers for alms-houses and work-houses, and leave poison to affect generations; and yet, so long as he commits no overt act so as to be taken red-handed, hands must not be laid on him, and if he comes to the law and asks for license to be married, the law gives it for the asking, and the judge with the dignity of his office, or the minister with prayers and benedictions, will perform the ceremony.

The same reasoning is applicable to the worthless, unbalanced creature that comes onto the plane of the hereditary pauper, too ignorant or worthless to secure food to live on, but with the ability to force upon the community a worthless and vicious posterity without limit as to number, and largely under the sanction of legal marriage. So of the high intelligence but criminal mentality that preys upon society and renders life and property insecure. So of the incurably diseased, the weak-minded, and those of insane tendencies. What rational distinction can be made between these and the leper in providing for the public safety? In the latter there is no wrong—only misfortune. Yet we claim the right to lay hands on him, put him away from his fellows, and perpetually exclude him lest he shall communicate his incurable affection to another. Why have we not equal right to lay hands on the others, isolate them, and prevent the spread of the contagion they will, otherwise, distribute far and wide? The plea of a "human soul" is lost here, for both have souls. On that line what becomes of the argument of the souls when the question comes before the church or the reformer, of why should these vicious classes be free to propagate their kind and bring into being millions of souls on the planes where all must be lost? Under what rule of logic or philosophy can you say to the law, "Hands off, the liberty of the person is sacred, the rights of the individual must not be interfered with," when, by isolating this one vicious body with a soul, you can prevent the production of many more vicious bodies with souls, all of which are likely or certain to be lost? The civil constitutions guarantee against only "unreasonable searches and seizures," and such as are made must be done in pursuance of law. Is such a seizure unreasonable in one case and not in the other? If the law authorizes one cannot it authorize the other?

And the Reformer; how shall he succeed in permanent reforms if he permits the constant production of subjects needing reform, when he is not now able to reform those existing, nor able to solve " the prison question?"

And the Law; how shall it continue to protect individuals and society, if it continues to license for marriage all who ask for license, and sanction as legitimate results of good government the constant production of these vicious classes? I do not mean malignant, but from which vice of various kinds inevitably breeds continually.

And Society; how shall it preserve moral purity or even ascendency, if it continues to hide behind a mask of false modesty and pride, and refuses to recognize conditions that exist, and refuses to build up and enforce a public opinion that by law will remove the causes that produce these conditions?

" Necessity knows no law," and " self-preservation is the first law of nature," are propositions as old as historical time. We recognize them in everything, except in this case of most vital necessity, this most certain danger of unrestrained marriage and indiscriminate propagation. · If self-defence is justified by law for the individual, it should be justified by law for society, in proportion that the importance of society is greater than that of the individual. If, to save life, limb and mortal injury, one may repel his assailant not only to disabling him, but to the taking of life, to save life, limb, and mortal injury, society may repel its assailants not only to the point of emasculation, but to the taking of life; and the policy that denies it is a cowardly policy, and the public opinion that does not enforce it is a false and cowardly one, and can produce nothing but injustice to the human race.

The final objection is, that such legislation as is suggested cannot be enforced.

Why not, as well and completely as any other legislation in support of public health and morals, and against public wrongs? Hundreds of statutory provisions exist for this purpose. Note a few. Any person, with intent to steal, who shall take, carry, lead, or drive away the personal goods of another, shall be deemed guilty of larceny, and a penalty is affixed. Any person who shall make any sale, assignment or transfer of property, with intent to defraud purchasers, or to hinder, delay or defraud creditors; and any person having knowledge of it who shall willingly make use of it, shall be deemed guilty of a misdemeanor, and a penalty is affixed. Any one who shall take, lead, carry, decoy, or entice away a child, to detain or conceal it from its lawful custodian; or who, being seventeen years old or over, has carnal knowledge of an insane woman; or whoever, while intoxicated, prescribes or administers medicine that endangers life; or whoever prescribes any secret remedy and refuses to make known what it is, if required, and so endangers life; or whoever administers any substance to produce miscarriage by a woman, or any woman who solicits any substance and takes it, or submits to any operation to produce a miscarriage; or any person who shall run a hand car on a railroad, not being an employee, without consent of the company; or whoever shall sell any diseased meat or other unwholesome provisions not fit for food, etc., etc., shall be deemed guilty of felonies, and penalties are affixed. Like provisions cover almost every kind of act that can injure property or person, for the protection of the state, corporations, the public and individuals. Many offenders are arrested, convicted and punished. Not all; and by this means crime has been held in check to some extent; many are deterred by it, and others are put out of harm's way for a greater or less length of time.

Now, suppose it should be made unlawful for any person to marry without procuring a license; and then providing how it might be procured; unlawful for any person to perform the marriage ceremony without license; unlawful to issue a license, or to marry any person within the prohibited class, the officer or person having knowledge at the time. Provide by law who shall not marry at all; say it shall be unlawful for any habitual drunkard, any person afflicted with incurable disease, or venereal disease, with hereditary scrofula, or who has been insane, or either of whose immediate ancestors died insane, any person afflicted with fits, any person of weak mind, incapable of providing for and taking care of themselves, any person who has been twice convicted of crime, any two persons who are both paupers and a public charge, any whose immediate ancestors were paupers and who have no visible means of support although not a public charge at the time, any person who is a

professional beggar, any person of notorious bad moral character, any abandoned person, or person living as a vagrant with
no visible means of support though not a public charge, shall
marry; or shall apply for license to marry; or shall live with
one of the opposite sex as if married; or shall become the
parent of any child; and affix a penalty. Require application
for license to be by petition, under oath, declaring that the applicant does not belong within any of the prohibited classes.
That any reputable person may object to the issue of license,
by statement in writing on oath, that one or both of the parties
belong within the prohibited class; on which, no license shall
issue until the question shall be determined. That after license,
like objection may be made at the time of the ceremony; on
which, the ceremony shall be suspended, and the license and objection be returned to the officer issuing it. Provide for a permanent and competent board of examination of applicants for
license. That applicants may apply for examination by the
board at their option before applying for license; and certifi-
cate shall issue to them of qualification if so found by the
board, which shall be presented with the application for license,
and shall be conclusive. When objection is made as above
specified, the officer shall lay the application before the board,
with the objection, and require the applicant to appear for examination. If on examination the board find the applicant
qualified, it shall return the papers with the finding and it shall
be conclusive. If they find the applicant within the prohibited
class, they shall order his commitment to the custody of the
sheriff, to be dealt with, as in cases of arrest on coroner's warrant. Provide a penalty for each and every violation by the
applicant, the officers, or board, and for any neglect of duty by
the officers or board, including perjury for false swearing by the
applicant, the objectors or any witness testifying before the
board. Make the board a body of inquest, with power to try
and determine the question of qualification. Make it felony
for any person to become the father of any illegitimate child.
If persons of weak mind become such parents, separate and
shut them up beyond the power of repetition. Let the penalty
for all violations include the incarceration of the offender in
some suitable prison for no determinate period, and to be re-

leased only on order of the board of pardons or parole, and so prevent repetitions of the offence. In severe cases, of rape, of syphilitic children, of assaults on insane women, or on girls, let the party be physically put beyond the power of repeating the offence, in the prison after incarceration, as a part of the penalty.

What difficulty would there be in enforcing such a law that is any greater than in the offences I cited, or in others? None —and not so much as in most others. Of course, all cases would not be reached; nor convictions follow in all cases prosecuted. Nor would it prevent marriage by all prohibited persons, nor wholly prevent illegitimacy. But as in other offences it would operate to deter crime in this direction; it would bring conviction for an average number of cases of violation equal to those for other offences. It would give every person desiring to marry ample opportunity. If not in the prohibited class the affidavit imposes no humiliation any more than the oath administered to a witness in court; nor the inquest any more than the challenge to a voter. The logic of an oath to a witness is this: " We do not know if you are entirely truthful. However you may be in fact, you swear in the fear of the law and its penalties that on this occasion, at this time, you will be entirely truthful." No man can take an official position until he takes an oath, and if his vote is challenged he cannot vote until he swears, and in some cases proves that he does not come within the prohibitions as to voters. So in this case. The law has a standing challenge as to applicants, for the protection of every person. It is no humiliation to pass the challenge by swearing the prohibitions do not apply, or to prove it if required; nor is it humiliating to voluntarily go before the board of examiners before applying for license, any more than it is to go before a board of registry before an election and secure a registry that will permit you to vote when you apply for that privilege. The way is open and easy to procure license to marry for all who would be entitled to it. More. Every decent person should be glad of such a protection against the grave dangers and boundless evils that all are subject to without such special effort for protection.

As to evidence of violation, it is no more hidden than in

other cases, and much less so than in most cases, and in all conspiracies. Incurable disease, insanity, imbecility, inebriety, and records of crime cannot be hidden, nor can a syphilitic or illegitimate child; pauperism and vagrancy are patent enough; and with the general condemnation in which such offenders are now held, certainly, there would be no public opinion seeking to shield them from prosecution, or to shield any one aiding, abetting, or assisting them in any way.

Therefore, the last objection must fall; and the odium of such conditions as now operate to fill the public institutions and prisons with an endless procession of diseased, deformed, demented and criminal inmates must rest upon general society, including the church, because within them lies all the power of a public opinion that can force this proper and necessary legislation, and enforce the execution of the laws when enacted.

The salvation of the morals of any nation is dependent upon the purity and health of its homes and domestic relations. Few ever think of the comprehensive meaning of that word "home." To many, it is only a mere domicile—a mere place to stay. But the true home, the home in fact, is the place where centers all that is most desirable and sacred in life; where every best impression is made; where memory turns to the fondest, the oftenest and the last; the place whence no bitter waters flow and where centers the strongest, the purest and the most lasting affections. Home, the true home, is the outgrowth of true love; the union of two mind energies of which I have spoken. This home is found only where there is a true marriage made by this union; and in such a home the divine essence of the love of the parents filters through the members of the family; and whatever of misfortune or poverty may overtake it, it will never be the voluntary source of hereditarily diseased or deformed bodies and minds. Such a marriage and such a home can be found only where there is intelligent mental force, and where the intellectual and moral forces dominate the animal impulses.

With such regulations as I have suggested, the true marriages and true homes would increase, with their ever widening benefits, and displace to the same extent the mere domiciles—

the places to stay—with their variant and unstable domestic associations; as often being mere tolerations as they are attractive cohesions.

And in addition, the mockery of marriage and the desecration of home perpetrated by the many, prompted not by love but by lust, would be fewer, and the vicious elements of mentality and physical deformity now undermining the morals and health of society, would gradually be lessened in volume and evil quality, and so lessen the labor of reformers, the burdens of government, and more than all, leave a chance and hope, for a coming generation sooner or later of purer blood, and indicate that humanity has as much interest in improving itself as it manifests in improving its domestic brutes.

CHAPTER VIII.

THE word society is variously applied to the association of human beings, from the smallest numbers associated to accomplish a common purpose, up through all kinds of unions until it takes in the general community, and is called the public. Again, in the several communities, the word is used to designate a particular portion, or set, that claim the exclusive right to the name as being *the* society in that particular community. I use the word in its most comprehensive signification, as meaning associated humanity, in the pursuits of life, in all the phases it presents. In this sense society is made up of the aggregated population, living in communities, as distinguished from individuals living apart from their fellows; and in speaking about it we must bear in mind the various conditions in, and influences exerted by, the various communities we find. To illustrate: In states having a local option law, some communities decide to have no retailing of strong drink, and none can be had. Those who want and will have strong drink, and believe in its free sale and disposition, must hunt another community to live in where the public option favors his views. So, the one community is subjected to the outgrowths, social, political and mental, that belong with prohibition, while the other is under those that belong with regulated license, or perfect liberty as to the use of spirituous liquors.

Or, take another case. The mental characteristics of the people and their environment may be such in one community as to produce a catholic spirit in regard to association. All may mingle together in common sociability; attending each other's socials, fairs, entertainments, and feasts, and mingling with sympathy in cases of misfortune and affliction; religious and political differences furnishing no barriers. In another community, they may be such as to divide the people into

small associations, or cliques, one having nothing to do socially
with any save the members of their own particular set. Another community may be noted for the educational, religious
and moral atmosphere that surrounds it, and shapes the
impulses and opinions of its members; while another may be
of that mentality and environment that is directly the opposite, abounding in places for drinking and gambling, amusements consisting of the lowest grade—racing, cock-pits, dog
fighting, prize fighting, etc., while education and theology find
a narrow margin on which to operate for reforms and social
and moral elevation, and where observance and enforcement of
moral and social laws are on a level with the other conditions.
To some extent the best and the worst elements are found in
every community; and to a lamentable extent the forces that
make the worst, are found on the levels where those move
who are possessed of abundant intelligence, and externally
present—as they socially represent—a high degree of morality.
The truly moral who occupy these levels find their influence
obstructed by that of their associates on the same level, who,
while being able to maintain their social position, are gratifying
immoral impulses, or accomplishing personal ends by immoral
methods, more or less masked from general observation, but
known to others on a lower level. It is from this intelligent
and pseudo-moral element in society at large that the influences and forces come that warp, misshape, and distort the
views of, and mislead and falsely educate the unbalanced mentalities on the lower levels, who might and would, otherwise,
be subject to and moved by good influences, or become less
immoral and dangerous.

Those on the lower social levels look to those on the higher
to learn; and they also look with feelings of envy; and they
sneer at all they find there making pretense of morality under
the garb of hypocrisy. One small spot of dirt when found is
spread all over the entire society, and the elevating influence
that might be felt otherwise is, to some extent, turned into an
evil one by finding some on the higher levels with no better
morals than there is on the lower. A truthful analysis discloses the lamentable fact that the criminal and immoral
classes are not confined to the lower social levels. Honesty,

morality, chastity, virtue and religious faith are found among
those on every level, and so are dishonesty, immorality, prosti-
tution and infidelity.   But those on the higher social levels
are more responsible than those below them, and should be
held to stricter account, because of their higher intelligence
and more favorable surroundings.   Were there fewer or no
reprobates moving in the best social circles, there would be
fewer among the worst ones.

An honest person of limited opportunities feels a constant
desire to better their condition.   One moved by purely selfish
motives will desire the same thing, no matter how much they
have already.   One without scruples will resort to any method
regardless of morals to the utmost boundary his fear of consequences will permit him to go.   One pressed by want, driven
by dire necessity, will pass all boundaries to relieve that necessity.   Offenders against the criminal law come from both of the
latter classes.   The first may be an intentional criminal, but
was made such by reckless pursuit of personal gain, meaning
to go as far as he could and not cross the criminal line, but
not hindered by any moral question of right.   The other is an
unintentional criminal, though he crossed the criminal boundary knowingly, driven by irresistible want.   The first case can
happen with one on any social level.   The latter cannot happen to any only those on the lowest level.   On the upper
planes are found those who are intelligent but with immoral
tendencies, and on the lower will be found those who are ignorant but with moral tendencies.   The latter are not unfrequently
made victims by the former, and made to suffer as criminals
though innocent of intentional wrong, being overreached and
misled because of their ignorance, by a misuse and abuse of the
higher intelligence of the former.

A minority of the people are professors of religion and a
majority are non-professors.   The former as a whole are believers in a Special Providence who can be persuaded by prayers, and they rely on that, mainly, as a force for the removal or
mitigation of the evils they encounter from the immoral classes.
Taking the religious professors' standard of morality, the majority of the people are not possessed of strong moral tendencies;
and taking the people at large the greater number have neither

time, opportunity, inclination or intelligence to study and become acquainted with social conditions and the problems that
social outgrowths present for solution. The efforts with all for
individual betterment, and of many for personal aggrandize-
ment, absorb the attention and exhaust their time and energies. There are three classes with which all others have little
patience or charity: and these are the dilatory, the unfortunate
and the rascally classes. In the aggregate they number largely,
and whatever adverse circumstances may happen to any of the
members they will lay the blame on some one besides themselves. The dilatory class lose advantageous opportunities by
waiting too long and by inattention to any business they may
have. The unfortunate classes seem born to misfortune and
are the victims of untoward circumstances they have no hand
in making, intentionally. The rascally class is by far the largest in numbers, and is such because its members have a mentality that finds a gratification in indulging its peculiar impulses, not to be found in any other way.

If a majority in society is moved by a common impulse, and
acts on it as a unit in giving utterance to its conclusions, it is
recognized as the public opinion. It is a force against which no
successful resistance can be made. An intelligent public opinion may be sometimes moved by fanatical impulses and is
dangerous and merciless. Or, it may be an ignorant public
opinion and it will possess the same character. An intelligent
and educated public opinion is likely to be moved by moral
impulses, but the intellectual and educated members of society
are in the minority as to numbers, and the members are often
so divided by matters of a purely personal character as to destroy the force it could exert in elevating every member of
society onto a higher plane, and so render invaluable service
for the entire body of the people.

A public opinion is not likely to form and make itself felt, unless the common moral sense is shocked in some way; or unless
some act or condition actually does, or threatens to, infringe
upon individual rights or interests generally. Society rarely if
ever takes cognizance of the actual conditions that exist within
and affect itself, as outgrowths of its organization. Individuals
here and there do so, and bring it to the knowledge of the

general public, and if there be a crisis impending growing out
of the conditions, a public opinion will form and assert itself.
It is owing to this indifference that so many evil conditions
obtain. In a conflict between the moral and animal elements
in society, the sympathy of the dilatory and unfortunate classes
are as likely to be with the latter as the former.

The reliance of the religious portion of society upon the interposition of Providence in answer to prayer, and the absorp-
tion of the time and attention of the other responsible members
of society in furthering their own interests, accounts for the
failure to recognize and study the causes that produce the evil
classes, and the formation of a public opinion directed to efforts
for the removal or modification of those causes.

As I have sought to show in the chapters on Mentality and
Natural Forces, the mentality and environment of the individual fixes the social plane he will occupy as a member of society,
and his impulses and acts will be the result of natural forces set
in operation by that mentality and environment. If his plane
is among the evil disposed, change of environment and change
of mentality must be effected to elevate him. I have sought
to show, in the chapter on Theology, that the superior can
elevate the inferior only by going to his level and bringing
itself within the comprehension of the inferior. The evil elements in society can be removed by only one of two methods:
elevation by change of mentality and environment, or by
physical force. It is within the power of the higher elements
of society to elevate the lower elements to some extent, but to
do this it must adopt such methods as will secure the attention
of the lower classes, and then, by individual and associated action seek to change mentality by enlightenment and change
environment by furnishing material opportunities. It will
make little headway as long as it tolerates customs and usages
on its own plane that are inconsistent with the elevated sentiments it professes and teaches. It cannot condemn and refuse
association with the mother of an illegitimate child while it
tolerates and associates with the father of it. It cannot condemn a swindler while it recognizes as a church communicant
one who, as a learned professional, resorts to questionable and
unscrupulous methods to defend and clear a guilty criminal. It

cannot be heard to preach morality, benevolence and charity, while the rich church members refuse to recognize as equals in the sight of God the poor but pious man and woman, who live upright lives and exhibit no distinction except in the lack of wealth. It cannot gain attention to exhortations about the sacredness of the rights of property, if it is making large profits and pinching labor to the lowest possible limits as to wages. It cannot gain the confidence of those it approaches, if, while rolling in wealth and luxury, it passes the poor and needy without recognition, or fails to reasonably minister to their wants out of its abundant substance. In a word, it can not preach one thing and practice another and expect to command the attention of those who indulge in evil practices. It must eliminate the evil-disposed elements in its own ranks as far as possible before becoming ministers of truth to those who lack moral perception on lower levels. The injunction of the Master, "first cast out the beam out of thine own eye, then shalt thou see clearly to cast out the mote out of thy brother's eye," is well understood and comprehended in principle by the meanest of mankind, though they may never have heard these words; and they are as ready to apply it to anyone subject to the challenge as was the Master to the hypocrites to whom he addressed it.

I said it had the power to elevate the lower classes; but it is hardly to be expected that the effort will be made. Individuals in it have labored for scores of years, and numbers of them in association have labored and are now laboring to that end ; but they cannot exert the force of a public opinion, and aside from the individual results of their own efforts they must rely on such municipal aid as they can persuade the law-making powers of the state to extend.

The unequal condition of society can never be removed solely by legislation. Much less can it be removed by class legislation; such as compulsory education, Sunday laws, prohibition of the manufacture and sale of spirits; so-called grants of special privileges, such as are granted to private corporations and associations, which are only pretended grants. In reality they are no grants at all. They are prohibitions of the exercise and enjoyment of individual rights by everybody ex-

cept those specifically named in the pretended grant. The
freeing of certain property from taxation while other property
is taxed. If a few rich men put their unneeded thousands into
a church it is exempt from tax; while the day laborer who puts
his hard earnings into a little dwelling on an out-lot, or the
farmer who raises a horse or cow, are taxed to the utmost, and
yet neither could get a seat in the church. A millionaire may
bequeath one and a half millions to a university already rich and
it becomes exempt from taxation. A poor man who has only
a horse and dray is taxed for the full value. A thousand in-
equalities that work injustice are tolerated and upheld by
society, while it has the power in its hands to correct them;
and as long as they exist the influence of its best moral elements will be badly handicapped in the efforts it makes to
elevate the lower classes by preaching morality and honesty to
them.

So long as society permits marriage to be regarded as an
amusement and divorce as a pastime, the evil-disposed will not
be impressed with any idea of sanctity in marriage. So long
as courts allow a man or woman to obtain three or more
divorces, having offspring with each marriage, which is separated with divorce, no one of the lower classes is going to
have any very elevated ideas of the value, the character, the
sacredness of a home. So long as a criminal can marry another criminal, join their wits and perpetrate crime in couples,
they will not have any special respect for the obligations that
belong to the marriage relations. So long as a man who is
barefooted is declared a felon and sent to the state prison for
stealing a pair of shoes, while the well-dressed man and woman
who conspire to and do extort money by blackmail and are
punished only as for a misdemeanor, the criminally inclined are
not going to have respect for the law or those who enforce it.
They know that the higher orders in society tolerate these
irregularities, and that not a few among their ranks commit
crime, indulge in immoral practices, and some of the most
successful, daring and dangerous criminals come from among
them. Highly educated and accomplished women, possessing
great wealth, and qualifications if rightly used to fill the highest places of influence and usefulness as wife, mother and

patroness of benevolent associations, run after, court, associate with and marry profligate men, both native-born and foreign, and men known to be such. And so-called good society in the cities, open their doors to these profligates who come here from abroad as mere adventurers, simply because they have titles or are born in titled families. As long as society tolerates and sanctions these customs and usages it is a serious question whether it can be called good society or is above the so-called lower classes in moral mentality. Certainly, but for the wealth it commands it would not be so regarded. I must not be understood as arraigning society or condemning it. I am merely referring to facts as they exist connected with it. And according to my philosophy it is a legitimate outgrowth of the mentality and environment of the individuals that make up society, under the operation of natural forces. And it is so because indiscriminate marriage and procreation is allowed, and practical knowledge is not used in rearing children.

When I come to speak of Legislation, of Convicts, of Punishment, and of Reformation, society with its conditions enters into the consideration as an important factor, as does each of the other subjects so far considered; and like the individuals to be dealt with, we must take it and them just as they are; and whatever propositions are made or presented must contemplate an adaptation to things and conditions as they exist; and as far as can be seen to such changed conditions as may follow the practical results of the propositions when carried into practice.

"The fountain can rise no higher than its source." The moral force exerted by society can only be such as the moral perception and conduct of its members possess and display. The communities and smaller associations and divisions of society present the alternating phases of good and evil. As before stated, one community will be highly moral while another will be grossly immoral. The standards of morality vary in different communities. In England they observe Sunday as a day for religious worship. In France it is observed as a day for sporting. In Germany part of the day is devoted to church and the residue to amusement. In Boston they observe Sunday, and in Chicago the theatres run as on week days.

Education and civilization are counterparts and alternately become cause and effect. The knowledge obtained through education, if properly used, begets true civilization, and that in turn begets a higher and true education. But if improperly used, it begets a false civilization, and that in turn may beget a higher, but it will be a false education. A true civilization is that which makes the best use of the opportunities that knowledge obtained by education discloses; while a true education is one that teaches us how to make practical use of knowledge and produce a mentality in which the moral impulses dominate, control and direct the animal impulses through the higher intellectual energies. A false civilization is that which misuses the opportunities education discloses and in turn begets and confirms a false education. Every advance made in the acquisition of knowledge, discloses new opportunities for practical advancement in some direction; and it always admits of use for individual and general good, and also for individual and general injury, directly or indirectly. If used for good ends, the outgrowth of that use leads to more knowledge, which discloses more opportunities that may be used in like manner. If used for evil ends, the outgrowth is more knowledge disclosing more opportunities, but the knowledge and opportunities are such as tend to and grow out of increasingly greater evils. The proper uses bring true civilization and education, and the improper use brings false civilization and education, This repetition is from an anxious desire to impress the reader, bearing in mind that environment and education make the impulses manifested by every mentality. Under the stimulating influences resulting from civil and religious liberty in this country, education and civilization have progressed rapidly, and on the whole towards a true civilization, until since the people have become numerous and the communities large. There was an instinctive obedience to law and a voluntary observance of order, while moral perception dominated in the mentality of a majority. Keeping pace with the increase of knowledge and opportunities has come the population until they crowd each other some and interests clash. With the misuse made of opportunities—especially in legislation, the acquisition of wealth, and the power it gives, and the importation of an undesirable and hetrogeneous population from abroad—it may be seriously questioned whether we are now making proper use of opportunities and whether improper use is not now producing a false education and a false civilization in turn ; and consequently, an obliquity of moral perception admitting of social conditions that finally end in a mentality leading to indifference to morals, and constantly adding to the numbers that are so rapidly increasing the defective and disorderly classes.

It cannot be unprofitable to briefly glance at a few facts in this connection, being evidences of the legitimate outgrowth of the use made of the increase of knowledge, and consider if the tendency is to a higher or lower moral perception. We will first look at the common school—so called. It is not possible for a poor boy or girl who cannot spare more than three months in a year to attend school, to obtain a knowledge of reading and writing and the fundamental rules of spelling, arithmetic and grammar, and so help them to study alone in what little leisure they can find between the demands on them for labor. As a fact, spelling and grammar and penmanship have ceased to be a part of a common school course. Writing is taught—or forced—but no effort is made to make a fair writer. They must go forward " with the class " from grade to grade, learn all that is allotted to that grade and take the next in order. There is no regulation by which a poor boy can devote so much time as he can spare to one study and then take up another. With a rudimentary knowledge of spelling, reading, writing, arithmetic and grammar, he could acquire enough knowledge to enable him to do ordinary business and acquaint himself with the current news of the day. But that is impossible ; and therefore, he must remain ignorant or depend on private help. The "graded system" has become so refined that the intention of the founders of the common schools, made free, with ample money to support them, where every child could secure the rudiments of a common education, leaving a higher order of culture to academies and colleges for such as desired to secure it, is entirely annulled and defeated. With ample public funds, and thousands desirous of taking advantage of just such provisions, there are no doors open to them. Out of one thousand children not ten in a hundred on

an average will become graduates of the "high school," and
yet it cannot be passed short of five years of hard labor, and
more money is expended to maintain it than for all the rest of
the pupils. The present graded system might all be well
enough, provided an arrangement were made so that those who
wished to acquire the rudiments of only a few branches could
do so, as rapidly as they could advance themselves. Learn to
read fairly, to write some, the ground rules of arithmetic and
something about spelling and grammar. If this is a proper
use of the opportunities opened by knowledge it is difficult to
comprehend it.

Or take the trades. Every door is closed against appren-
tices. It is next to impossible for a youth to acquire a trade.
A man may not teach his own son the trade he follows. He
must first obtain the consent of the "union" in which his
trade is classed, or else the boycott and ostracism will destroy
him. That is not easy to obtain; the argument being lest the
supply of workmen in the trade increase beyond the demand
and so decrease wages.

Or in another direction. The division of labor renders it
nearly impossible to acquire a knowledge of one line of business. One man cannot make a boot, or shoe, or plow, or hoe,
a suit of clothes, a wagon, a wheelbarrow, a bureau, a chair, or
bind a book; and so on throughout the trades. One person
works at one piece, one at another, and when the parts are
completed, different persons put different parts together. So
that many persons take part in completing a simple thing and
no one can work at another's part or make the whole himself.
So in merchandise. Goods are all classified and each class is
graded and no one person handles or sells only one class and
one grade. It is gloves and of a certain grade, laces, fans,
silks, woolen goods, and so on, through endless classifications,
and one person has no general knowledge of a common or
general stock, but only of one particular line. If employment
is lost, unless they can find another opening in the same class
or line, they are helpless and have no chance to labor when
they are willing and have need to. Capitalists establish and
carry on the business. Foremen are hired for every department. In a house with hundreds of employés, perhaps not

twenty have any general knowledge of the business and no opportunity to acquire it. Much the same condition of affairs exists among common manual laborers; and any attempt of new men to acquire situations, or knowledge of any kind of work so as to labor at hard work in any kind of employment, is met with opposition by those already in, and great difficulty is found in obtaining a chance to convert muscular exertion into the means to appease hunger. Let any one visit the labor agencies where thousands come during every month inquiring for chances to perform hard manual labor at almost anything, and they can realize something of the truths I am trying to impress.

In another field, legislation in every law-making department of government—national, state and municipal has made invidious distinctions until almost a system of class enactments have place in the public statutes, as well as the regulations of private corporations, all of which are within the jurisdiction of the courts for enforcement. A man may not take interest beyond a certain sum per cent. per annum, nor may any one contract to pay more, no matter what the need for money and when it cannot be obtained at that rate. By being permitted to pay what is demanded a borrower might save himself from bankruptcy perhaps in some cases. And this restriction is made in the interest of morals and to prevent oppression by lenders in times of stringency. But, being unable to borrow the money at the legal rate of interest, judgment and execution go and the man's property is seized. Now, the creditor may take, and the borrower may pay any sum without limit— one thousand per cent. per day—to secure forbearance of execution or sale. He may not give what he is willing to give for a loan to tide over an emergency and prevent judgment and execution, lest the lender be wicked and oppress him. But when he is oppressed, the creditor may be as wicked as he likes, and the borrower may pay what he likes, though he may be much more oppressed thereby. Or, in case three men enter into partnership and become indebted, the property of the firm and of each partner can be seized to pay the debt. It would be immoral to be allowed to escape liability as individuals although credit was given to the firm only, as a firm. But let the same three men declare themselves a corporation and file the declaration in a public office designated, and then become indebted, creditors can look only to the corporate property for the debts.   Each individual may be worth a million and not a cent can be reached.   The morality in these distinctions is hard to find ; the injustice is patent.

Again, government will sell a tract of land and issue to the buyer a patent, and covenant to warrant and forever defend him in the title and possession against all claimants.   The buyer improves that land, builds a dwelling and other conveniences, spends years and rears a family there, builds up associations and memories dearer than life, expects to die and be buried there and leave it as an inheritance for his children. Some few other persons declare themselves a corporation to build a railroad and they run the line to suit themselves, and it goes through this person's dwelling and land.   They desire a part of the land to take gravel from and another part to waste dirt on.   The owner refuses to sell and destroy his home and the associations and memories of a lifetime, and go away to build up a new one in his advanced age.   That government, in violation of its warranty, tranfers the right of eminent domain to those few men who are seeking their own personal gain, and under a law made for that purpose by that same government, its warranty is annulled, the land and home is condemned, not for public but for private use, and those persons take it by force from the owner, and drive him out to begin anew.   And nothing is considered except the market price of the property compared with other land that is offered for sale in the locality.   A grosser case of tyranny, injustice, bad faith and oppression can hardly be conceived, and no other country than this practices it.

Nearly all laws for indirect taxation operate unequally and unjustly, and the statutes contain very many enactments of class character creating unjust and oppressive distinctions.   It would seem to be quite evident that this is not such a use of the opportunities created by knowledge as tends to a true civilization, and in its turn bringing a higher knowledge as true education, that will open still greater opportunities.   But rather, it is such a use as begets a sense of injustice, an abuse

of power, and the operation of natural forces resulting, tend
toward a lower plane, a lower moral perception, the evolving
of feelings of contempt for law and disbelief in justice. In a
word, it begets a false civilization, in turn begetting a false
education.

One more illustration will be sufficient. Political parties are
the result of variance in opinion on questions of policy in
government. But such use has been made of this knowledge
as to create partisan clans in the place of political parties, and
they are miscalled political parties. The personal partisan
spirit took the place of the patriotic spirit, and the citizen,
whose duty it was to consider proposed policies as to their
benefit and utility in government, both projected and considered policies not in that light, but as a matter of partisan
expediency to attract voters and secure possession of the government offices. This use of opportunities led to the enfran-
chisement of newly landed foreigners, and the extension of the
elective franchise to persons not citizens, and to others, until
many ignorant and degraded elements of society actually held
the balance of power at the ballot box. That led to the
practice of bribing and tampering with deposited ballots and
election count and returns, and at this time there are in every
state plenty of voters, with their ballots in the market as a
commodity, for sale to the highest partisan bidder, to the
number of from 5,000 to 50,000 in some localities. Of course
the honestly expressed will of the majority of the voters is
never the result of elections, and the benefits expected from a
government by the people are not attainable. This use of
opportunities has, through the operation of natural forces, developed a moral perception that guides the administrators of
government in a like direction; and in the formation of legislative committees, the making and enforcement of rules in
legislation, the appointments to subordinate offices, and the
general conduct of public affairs, the use of opportunities
afforded by knowledge are directed to the perpetual retention
of power in the hands of the partisans holding it, and the exclusion of opponents, regardless of the will of a majority of the
honest voters of the nation.

This demoralizing influence filters down from the high

official places and taints the entire body of society; and the
methods are introduced into petty local selections in associations non-political. In the glaring instance just noticed no
one can be blind to the fact that, the knowledge given by education is prostituted to base uses; and in turn, creates opportunities which, being availed of in like spirit, begets knowledge
that tends to further base uses, and so a true education and a
true civilization may be rendered impossible, and when true
they will be perverted and made false.

As yet, the judiciary have mainly escaped the baneful influence of partisan strife, although in some instances the poison has manifested itself and is being spread by partisan nomi-
nation and election of partisan judicial officers; but there has
been such uses made of opportunities in connection with the
administration of justice, that faith in the wisdom, justice and
equity of the courts is materially weakened, and respect for
the law and its methods has sensibly diminished. These conditions in society are patent to the commonest mind; and the
abuse of knowledge, and the misuse of opportunities knowledge creates, by many of those on the higher social planes is
construed by many of those on the lower moral planes as example and license; and so, under the operation of natural
forces the great law of equilibration brings upon society the
burdens of crime, perverted mentality and increasing pauperism, and charges the higher orders with responsibility for it.
It is in the face of these facts, which should be known to all of
ordinary intelligence, that philanthropists and reformers approach those needing reform and attempt to understand and
solve "the prison question."

The social conditions in the former slave states demand some
consideration.

Two distinct races of different physiological organism—
physical and mental—of entirely different mentality and mentalism, are living together. The white race is the progressive
race, the authors and creators of all the education and civilization that exists. The black race is a non-progressive and
purely imitative race. Every practical idea possessed by every
member of that race above the level of the barbarian, is one
originated by the white man. The language, the productive

means for living, the customs and social regulations, the forms of government, the rights to and means of protection as to persons and property, and every element that enters into civilization are emanations from the ingenuity and intelligence of the white race. So long as the colored race are connected with and not separated from the white man it can follow him; it is not only incapable of leading, but, if left to itself, removed from that connection and association, it begins to retrograde, and in one century will lose all it has learned and finally relapse into its normal condition of barbarism. The brain structure of the colored man with its source of supply is of such a character that he cannot retain progressive intelligence and energy when left to himself. Even when with the white man in large bodies, the education he acquires is more largely used in gratifying purely personal impulses than in efforts to elevate and advance in a general line of progress. His nature is essentially animal and emotional, and not intellectual. His moral ideas are wholly emotional and his religion a tangible thing that he can feel somewhere, as he would a lump in his throat or an overloaded stomach. Philosophy and reason play no part in either—they are born of emotional impulse.

An admixture of white man's blood tends to give him higher moral perceptions. Scholastic education elevates him in mental power, and in close juxtaposition with the white man, with his example to follow and his means to use, he reaches the highest level he is capable of attaining; but left to himself he is incapable to retain his advanced place, and his successive generations deteriorate and drift back to his normal non-progressive level. The isolated cases of marked elevation in intelligence that occur, argue nothing and prove nothing against this view, and the conclusion defies successful contradiction. Noted men have arisen among them, noted educational institutions are maintained by them, but they are founded on, conducted by, and entirely dependent on resources furnished by the white man, and are located in the midst of white men and their institutions. They have never been tried in any case where dependent on their own intellectual resources. Toussaint L'Overture, one of the highest types of French half-blood, did something for his race, but the results of his efforts

are lost in the inevitable retrogression to semi-barbarism, and
it is still going lower. Dumas and Fred Douglass, the two
highest types next, perhaps, did nothing for their race. They
received a white man's education, in a white man's school,
lived among white men, married white wives, and did nothing
other than to advance as individuals in imitation simply of
white men, as followers and not leaders,

In the northern states the scattered negro population give
us individuals that reach a respectable level in use of a white
man's opportunities and surroundings; while as a rule, the
larger number use their opportunities to gratify the animal
and emotional impulses, rather than the intellectual impulses
for the elevation of the man. Remove the restraints of a white
man's government and the race would divide into clans and
tribes, and descend to the level that belongs to the contentions
and tyranny of tribal conflict. It argues nothing to say they
have had no chance. They have had the same chances the
white race has had and for the same length of time. Nor does
it argue anything to say there are ignorant, degraded and non-
progressive persons among white men. As a race the whites
are progressive ; as a race the blacks are non-progressive. The
former create opportunities for advancement. The latter do
not ; and when given possession of the white man's and left to
himself, loses them.

For two centuries the black occupied the position of forced
personal subordination, and the mental perceptions of the
southern white man of the true relations that exists between
the races was the outgrowth of that environment, and of the
education it brought. For a quarter of a century the black
has been released from that position, and by the fiction of
legal enactment occupies a political and social level with the
white ; but in reality, he was placed, and is under a worse
domination and subordination, because his position makes a
white or black civilization imperative, and the whites will
never permit the latter. Led by his own impulses, unguided by
reason because of his ignorance of conditions and their causes,
incapable of comprehending the natural and social relations, he
is forced into a continual antagonism, the outcome of which
must end in his deportation or annihilation, sooner or later.

Miscegenation exists to some extent, but it leads directly to hybridism. The white man is willing to extend to the black all of his own opportunities, but he will not fraternize with him. There are no harmonious elements or outgrowths to bring them together, and there are incradical elements and outgrowths to keep them apart as two distinct races, and inharmonious elements cannot dwell together as equals. The white man is willing to create property, pay taxes, maintain schools and government, and give the negro the advantages of education; to protect his person so long as he observes the public order, and allow him to do business and acquire for himself. But with all this he knows that, as a race, the black cannot use them. With individual exceptions, their moral perceptions are obtuse, and honesty and chastity are "more honored in the breach than in the observance." In these respects they are not different from many in the white race; but they lack progressive energy and perception, and the animal impulses govern them to such an extent that the tendency is toward a lower plane. This is evidenced by the fact already cited, that in the prison population the blacks exceed the whites in proportion of five or six to one and the increase comes largely from the blacks that have had the benefit of more or less education. Other instances can be cited.

In the northern states there are political demagogues who, for partisan ends, regardless of anything else, are determined to maintain the negro on a political and social level with the southern whites, in order to make sure of his vote to keep their party in power. This leads to impractical and oppressive legislation inimical to the whites, and breeds more antagonism, and a resort to questionable methods to evade the operation of the unwise enactments. Another class of northern people, properly termed sentimentalists, desire to regard the negro as a "brother," and persist in efforts to teach him he is such, for "God made of one blood all the nations of the earth;" and, like the negro, with no real knowledge of the actual social conditions in the south, and as little consideration of the natural forces relating to mentality and its outgrowths, and those growing out of the forced mingling of inharmonious elements, they stimulate and make active only the impulses.

that lead to antagonism instead of harmony. Between the two, the negro is "between the devil and the deep sea;" the devil of his own ignorance and non-progressive nature, and the deep sea of the superiority of the white race he is surrounded by, which is able to prevent his becoming the superior, will not recognize him as an equal, simply because he is not, and the relation of equals cannot be either established or maintained.

There are many intelligent, good, moral and excellent persons among the blacks; but I speak of them as a race, and that cannot be said of them as a race. Like Sodom, there are not enough righteous among them to save them from the fate that awaits them beyond any power to prevent. In consequence of these facts, the prison question presents some features that do not belong to it in the northern states; and the same method of conducting prisons and efforts for reform of convicts will not apply there in all respects, that would be possible at the north. A different classification and different kind of treatment and teaching is necessary, and the true consideration is possible only to southern white people who have actual daily knowledge of and experience with local social conditions. These conditions are anomalous and cannot be met in the prison question in the south as we would deal with conditions in the north. They require a more careful study of the operation of natural forces applicable to the inequality of the races and the peculiar environment; a modification of the standards of right and wrong; a more liberal view as to the standard of morals; and a greater use of physical force. These views may not be palatable or popular and will be rejected by many; but they are true, and we must recognize them as being so and deal with conditions accordingly, or they will deal with us to our injury.

The inequality in the distribution of the fruits of labor, and the results from the relations of capital and labor as capital is managed, being such conditions as tend to and produce criminals and crime, and it might be expected that the subject would be noticed in connection with other social conditions. The subjects of Labor, Capital and Property with their so-called "rights" and relations to the individual and the community, are material factors in a full consideration of the subject of crime and its causes, and to many it may seem of importance in discussing the prison question; but it has not seemed so to me. The prison question properly deals with the disposition of criminals as well as removing the causes of their production; and as class legislation of every character produces the conflict that exists between capital and labor, from which grow the conditions that tend to make crime and criminals as one cause, the condemnation of such legislation is sufficient in discussing the prison question. To enter the field and undertake to discuss the economic questions relating to labor, capital and property, is a distinct and voluminous work by itself. It is claimed that every man should be "permitted to live out his own life," and that this is the very essence of liberty; subject, however, to necessary restrictions to preserve order; and to do this the right to property is a natural right under the moral law. But that the property should be used for the good of all and not of one alone. When the owner has realized all that he needs out of it, he should use the rest for the common good. This is correct enough in morals, but not practical in fact, because man will regard morals as he does everything else—so far as he can make it useful to himself and his accumulations. The only practical legal remedy for equalizing pecuniary conditions, lies in the direction of so providing that all have equal opportunities, and that taxation bears equally on accumulations. If government grants a franchise, such as for a railroad, canal, street cars, lighting, water supply, gravel, toll or other kind of road, or of any kind, it should reserve control, fix the limit of charges, reserve a portion of the revenue, prohibit accumulations beyond a proper limit, allow the operators a fair income, a reasonable surplus for contingencies, and take the overplus; and reduce the charges for service when the income increases beyond a fair and reasonable limit. No monopolies should be allowed, except such as are conducted and controlled by government for purposes of revenue to itself; and the accumulations to ownership in land should be limited so as to prevent private monopoly in it. No special privileges should be conferred that benefit some and burden others. In "living one's own life" the acquisition of property is a matter not readily controllable. One who cannot judiciously use the opportunities his position gives, cannot acquire property, or keep it if given to him. Others are so constituted that they will not do so when they can. Others who have opportunities and commence to accumulate are not able to control conditions, and are forced to arrange for constantly increasing accumulations. Men in business with liberal incomes, make investments, and competition, new inventions, fluctuations of markets, new discoveries of material, and other things, compel great enlargements, and of necessity the business and accumulations continue to grow. It would be bankruptcy to stop and contraction without disaster is impossible. Or, on the other hand, want of sufficient capital prevents extension and a suspension becomes inevitable. Or again, one having enough retires from business on permanent investments. Change in securities may bring a largely increased income and require still other investments, and without any intention of enlargement of income he may become the center of a sort of pecuniary maelstrom where wealth flows in upon him. On the other hand, depreciation in securities from various causes may leave him without income. These things are dependent on the rights of persons and things as the law and social usages now recognize them. The whole matter of property rests in three things as I have sought to show: the peculiar mental perception of the individual that enables him to so use opportunities as to acquire, keep and judiciously use money, property and labor. With humanity as it is, no amount of preaching or teaching will effect much change in its moral ideas about property. The man who can accumulate and keep while "living his own life," is not going to throw anything away or give away what he is not compelled to, to enable some other man to "live his own life." Men who have, will expend or give where their impulses may dictate, and not because of any view to equalize conditions. While a large amount of crime could be prevented by a proper and equitable limitation of individual accumulations—now permitted by means of special privileges conferred through class legislation—on one hand, and the offering of large opportunities to many now deprived of them by the abrogation of that kind of legislation, on the other hand, such a consummation can be reached only through the force of a healthy and moral public opinion. Until that grows and asserts itself, the factors to be considered in the prison question must be considered, dealt with, and used, without including the "labor problem." In other words, we must endeavor to take conditions as they are, and ameliorate, improve and reform where possible, and not attempt to change conditions that can only be changed by like processes to those that produced them. They are things of growth from seed sown by contingencies, not controllable until they fully develop their character and origin, and can be changed only by gradual progress as the successive generations follow each other.

CHAPTER IX.

THE duties of government are, to preserve public order, protect each person—natural and artificial—in their rights of personal franchise and property, administer justice, and leave each person in the enjoyment of the fruits of his own skill and labor, and in the enjoyment of the largest personal liberty consistent with the rights of others and of the general public welfare; taking of the substance of each, under equal and just laws, so much as in the aggregate will pay the expenses of government, honestly and economically administered, and no more. The government in this country is exclusively one of law. The objects, ends and aims to be attained by laws for government, are expressed by the preambles to the constitution of the United States and of the several states. While they slightly vary in words, they use language conveying substantially the same idea in all. That to the federal constitution declares it to be, "to establish justice, insure domestic tranquillity, provide for the common defence, promote the general welfare, and secure the blessings of liberty to ourselves and our posterity." That of one of the states says, "to the end that justice be established, public order maintained and liberty perpetuated." To enact such laws as will secure these ends, or tend to secure them, and to honestly and fairly enforce them, is the duty of the representatives of the people in the various constitutional departments provided for the purpose of administering government.

Governments are like individuals, and are subject to like influences and the operation of natural forces. The mentality of government can never be better or greater than is that of the persons chosen to organize and administer it; nor can its laws be any more just and wise in formation and effect, than is the perception of wisdom and justice in the minds of the legislators; nor can they be executed with any more fairness and justice than will be dictated by the moral sense of justice within the minds of those entrusted with that duty, from the governor and highest judicial functionary down through every official to the lowest grade of administrative officers.

The delegated and implied power of government has the force of unanimous public opinion, provided with means to enforce compliance with its dictates or demands, as between it and the people subject to it; being regarded as the will of the majority of the people expressed according to the forms prescribed by law, yet, the intelligence and ethical force contained in municipal law will correspond with the intelligence and moral perceptions of the general body of the people whose representatives enact it. But when it comes to the enforcement of the law upon individuals, the manner and efficiency of the execution, and the effects as a means for governing the people, will depend upon the intelligence and moral perceptions of the body of the immediate community in which the enforcement is attempted.

The efficiency of law as a means for effecting the duties and objects of government, depends upon the justice it effects when enforced, and upon the promptness and certainty with which it is enforced. Unless the public opinion is satisfied with the justice of the law it will not sustain it; and unless it be promptly and certainly enforced it will be regarded with indifference even if just. Especially will this be so with the criminal, and with the public as to criminals. The law specifically defines the acts that shall be considered as crimes and in disturbance of public order and fixes penalties; and it prescribes a code of procedure for executing the law and inflicting penalties. When one commits an offense against this law the relation between him and government becomes twofold; partaking of the nature of master and servant, and also of guardian and ward. Government takes the custody of his person and has the right to command him and enforce obedience. At the same time it must give and secure to him his rights under the law and protect him in the exercise of them, and furnish the means to enforce them for his own benefit. In bailable cases he may give bail and go at large until convicted and sentenced.

He may waive bail and have his writ of right to inquire into the cause of his detention. He may demand that a copy of the accusations against him be given him, and that they shall be so certainly stated that a charge of the same acts cannot be repeated in any form in another accusation after trial on them. He may require the names of the witnesses against him and that they testify in his presence in court. That he may be tried by a jury of citizens, with a reasonable chance to object to those he may not want to sit; to have the benefit of counsel; and compulsory proceess to bring his own witnesses into court. These, with other rights, government must enforce in his favor, and require its prosecutor who appears on behalf of the people, to recognize him as one of the people entitled to protection as well as every other person in the state; and see to it that a fair and unprejudiced presentation of the facts is made, and a fair hearing given; and that he is to stand as innocent of the offence charged until his guilt be established by evidence. In all this the government is his guardian, while holding him in custody as his master. When convicted, sentenced, and infliction of the penalty begins, and thence on until ended, government is still guardian, and must see to it that its officials are not actuated by any vindictive spirit, or inflict the penalty with any views of vindictive justice; but that it be done with a purpose to reform the criminal and induce him to thereafter obey the law and observe the public order. While as his master it holds him, commands his services, and enforces obedience, as his guardian it must also protect him, provide for his necessities and health, and seek to aid him to secure his own future welfare as a law-abiding citizen. The fundamental law contemplates that the code "shall be founded on principles of reformation and not vindictive justice."

The action of government relating to offenders has been a matter of growth, with constant modifications in favor of the offender; but at no time has the law-making power seemed to have actually grasped this true idea of the relations between the criminal and government, and practically legislated with those relations in view to carry into practical effect the expressed intendment and command of the constitution. "The principle of reformation" is to be the foundation of all enactments under which government may deal with the criminal. A "principle" is a rule of action growing out of an existing condition of facts. When the condition ceases the principle no longer exists. "The principle of reformation" growing out of the condition of facts that exist when one becomes a criminal and government takes him into custody to restrain him and make him feel the power of government to inflict a penalty, and to perpetually isolate him from society if it wills to do so, demands such legal provisions by government as will secure the safe custody of the offender beyond the possibility of escape, such management as will impress upon him the value and benefit of good and regular habits and useful labor, while it endeavors to cultivate such a mentality as will give him moral perception, and a mental balance that will enable him to be guided by it; and to retain him in custody until such balance is obtained. If it be found impossible to give him a balance, then to hold him in custody as an element unfit to be at large. The "principle of reformation" extends beyond him, and if he cannot be reformed himself he should not be allowed to contaminate others. Under this principle the operation of natural forces at once creates the relations of master and apprentice between government and the criminal, for government is entitled to his services and has the right to command him until he is fit to go out for himself as an orderly, obedient citizen; and also that of guardian and ward, for government is charged by the law with the duty of making such provisions as are possible, to educate and train the criminal to a mental level where he will regard obedience to law as a moral obligation, and so be entitled to the blessings of liberty, personal and political.

This constitutional duty imposed upon government, seems to have been misunderstood; and the provisions made have overlooked the actual necessities required in order to found the penal code on the principle of reformation. The reason for this, perhaps, may be found in the fact already stated, that criminal legislation has been a matter of growth, successively founded on preceding enactments, without any special effort to consider the matter philosophically. For instance, penalties have been prescribed as *punishment* for offences; they

were fixed and determined without regard to any reform.
And when inflicted, the offender was restored to liberty and
citizenship, regardless of the fact whether he was morally better or worse than when taken into custody. It was as if a
banker found his cashier stealing money and should suspend
him, shut him up a couple of years or more, support him, teach
him a trade, and at the end of the term put him back as cashier, regardless of the fact whether he was less or more of a
thief than when suspended. A moment's consideration of the
constitutional requirement will disclose that such a code could
not be the one intended and required, and such laws as were
made and now largely obtain could not be "founded on the
principle of reformation."

Every statute law should be founded on and embody a principle applicable to the subject matter, to perpetually remain as
long as the law exists, whatever modifications or changes may
be made in it. To illustrate: If the legislature concludes to
make a general incorporation law, under which private corporations can organize and become invested with corporate rights
and powers, it should be based on and contain a principle em-
bodying the intent and spirit of the law, that should be perpetual. That no rights should vest that would deprive the
law of as complete control over it as it exercises over natural
persons; no business should be conducted other than that
named in the articles of incorporation ; no enlargement of capital be allowed without permission of the legislature; no consolidation with other corporations be allowed without like permission ; no formation of subordinate corporations by the same
members within and subject to the main corporation for any
purpose; and no corporation should be organized for longer
than a term to be fixed by law, or be renewed on expiration
without legislative consent, and on dissolution the officers and
stockholders should be responsible for all debts and liabilities.
(I cite these by way of illustration). Changes in social, business
and political conditions, may render modifications of this gen.
eral law necessary ; but the principle—the heart—should re.
main and all changes be in accordance with it.

Bearing this in mind, we will take this constitutional direction as to the criminal code, and every proposed statute,

whether made to-day, next year, or at any future time, should look to the end to be accomplished by law, and endeavor to know the conditions existing at the time of enactment, the rule of action growing out of them, and what rule of action will arise as a natural result under the conditions as affected by the proposed law; and then, so frame the statute as to preserve the constitutional principle and make the operative force of the statute tend to the end designed.

If the theories presented in the preceding chapters are really theories, if they agree with the environments, then there are principles that should govern the preparation of laws, and be recognized by government in its enforcement of them as to criminals. Under those principles all ideas of punishment by the state for the offence should be laid aside. The idea of so providing as to effect reformation if that be possible, becomes the principle—the heart of every enactment. The government, in effect, says to the criminal: "There can be no liberty, no justice, no government, without public order, and safety for persons and property. From some cause you disregard this truth and disturb the public order and trespass on persons and property, and defy government. Therefore, you must be taken from society and be placed in confinement until it can be assertained why you are an enemy to order. If you can be so changed as to voluntarily observe and help maintain order, you can be released; if not, you must remain in confinement. It will depend wholly on yourself which will result." With this understanding the offender goes into close custody of the keepers and teachers provided by government, and the practical operation of the provisions made for reformation will begin. These provisions will include proper places for safe keeping; proper classification of offenders, on different bases and for different reasons and purposes; proper provisions for labor, physical and mental examination and culture; in a word, pathological treatment looking to the creation of a mental balance, while the delinquent is made to earn the expense he puts the government to on his behalf as far as possible; for strict discipline without cruelty or injustice; and such provisions for a hearing on his behalf by the supreme authority as shall convince him that justice is intended and within his reach at all times; that if he becomes reformed he can be restored to liberty; if not, he will remain in custody. These things will be further considered when I come to speak of punishment and prisons. The object now is, to show that government has not considered the true relations between itself and the criminals, and has not regarded the constitutional injunction in the preparation and enforcement of its criminal code. It has not made proper use of the opportunities afforded by the knowledge gained by education, and has produced a false civilization in regard to the criminal classes. The operation of natural forces under the legal provisions it has made, has created a false education in regard to crime and punishment: which, in turn, has operated to work injustice, and that in turn has begotten distrust of the law in the orderly and led to the appeal to Judge Lynch in all communities, on the one hand, and contempt in the disorderly for all claims of justice in the law as administered through the courts, on the other hand. It has given rise to all the complications that are now involved in the prison question. It has disregarded the *causes* of existing conditions and created forces that so operate as to aggravate and magnify those causes, and so make the conditions worse. It has brought into action other forces which, retroactively, have obstructed all practical legislation in the line heretofore followed. As in the case of the false issue created by the labor element; evolving a baseless sentiment that has driven labor out of many of the prisons and turned criminals in idleness into maniacs; and in another line made legislation necessary that is alike unjust and injurious to the government and the criminal. It has created an impractical and unreasonable sentimentality in society, the outgrowths of which have made a mockery of the theory of punishment, and heroes of the worst offenders. Recently, through the indefatigable efforts of reformers, and driven by the necessities of the situation, in some localities, government is beginning to comprehend its true relations toward the criminal, and efforts are being made to to make provisions "based on the principles of reformation."

The economic interest of government in the legal provisions, and their proper enforcement, relating to criminals, is very im-

portant and cannot be overestimated.   It is not one simply of
mere dollars and cents as an item of government expense, but
of a far greater monetary cost, in addition to the social and
moral consequences.   The expense to government can be very
largely diminished by proper and careful legal provisions; and
the saving to the community at large in safety to persons and
property will be many fold greater than that to government.
The warden, physician, and chaplain of a prison, should be
chosen for their superior abilities and requirements for the
special duties required of them in their positions.   Especially
should the physician be from among the ablest in his profession.   Not merely a man to prescribe for the bodily ailments
as a doctor, but one who can elevate both body and mind in
strength by proper hygienic and physical rules and practice.
The chaplain should be a man of broad catholicity; unhampered by special creed or dogma; one who can grapple with
conditions and use them for the purposes contemplated by the
law.   If the chaplain finds a man who is so constituted that he
cannot comprehend a special Providence, or the Christian idea
of a soul and its salvation, he should be able to find what
moral anchorage there may be, if any, and by that try to hold
his pupil to a perception of right, as the best for himself.   If
he can find nothing but the gross superstitions that govern
dense ignorance, then be able to use them as a means for control, by stimulating a fear of evil and a hope of good through
their operation, adapted to his mentality.   The warden should
be equal to either in capacity, and should be educated to his
business.   He should be of even temper, firm, fearless, of suave,
kindly manner, and one able to establish and maintain discipline, and conduct business with good executive and administrative ability.   These men should be placed above the reach
of temptation and want, and once located their place should be
permanent so long as they properly fill it.   The results to the
public from the proper action of each, would be more important than is that of any judge of a court, and the dignity, compensation, and value of the position should be recognized as
belonging on the highest plane occupied by officials.   It is a
gravely mistaken action that makes the selection dependent on
a partisan political policy, and a matter of cheapness of com-

pensation, and of "letting" to the lowest bidder, on one or more of which bases it has been too often put. Government has no more important responsibility on it than that involved in providing for the unbalanced classes among the people subject to it ; and the highest intelligence it can command should be called into its service in making and maintaining those provisions. These classes as social and political factors place government in position of one who has to use a candle for a light, and is compelled to keep it lighted at both ends. While they disturb order and entail danger and expense themselves, they propagate others of like disposition, and contaminate still others who might be orderly but for them. It is, therefore, the best economy to secure the highest order of ability in caring for those in being, and prohibit the propagation and contamination of more, so far as human foresight will permit.

CHAPTER X.

LEGISLATION AND THE CRIMINAL.

THE legislation in this country in relation to crime and the disposition of criminals has been an unstudied and unreflecting matter of law-making; formerly based on the impulses of those taking an interest in such legislation rather than on reasoning, and afterward the following along in the old ruts, adding to it as change of social conditions seemed to call for an increase in the list of acts to be made criminal. The great body of the law is the common law of England, adopted and made the law in this country. There were many common-law offences, but in the United States most generally, it was provided that crimes must be statutory, and no act could be treated as criminal except such as should be declared crime by statute. Statute must specifically define what acts should constitute crime and affix a penalty. In some states portions of the common-law offences were retained and might be prosecuted as at common law. The penalty was to *punish* the offender and so deter him from further offending, and by example deter others who might be disposed to offend. With this idea all penalties were fixed and determinate. If they failed to deter the offender they were repeated and perhaps increased. Formerly they were severe, but were gradually modified. Prisons were conducted as matters of speculation, and the effort was made to make them self-supporting or a source of profit to the state. The criminal was to be regarded as infamous and the badges of it were to attach to him. No thought was taken for anything but to make the criminal suffer in body and mind as punishment, and so create a mere animal fear to again offend. A large discretion was left to court and jury as to the penalty, which was generally on a sliding scale with maximum and minimum limit, to inflict the whole or any part above the minimum. While in the motives of the criminal there would be no difference, the law would make distinctions in the offence and penalty in some cases, but none in another. As instance in larceny: While the motive and act was to steal, if the value taken was under a certain sum it was petit—or little—larceny, if over that sum it was grand larceny. The former might be punished as a felony or as a misdemeanor, and the latter as a felony only. In assault and battery the penalty might be a fine of from one cent to one thousand dollars, with or without imprisonment in jail. In trespass to real property the fine could not exceed twice the value of the property injured and no mention of malice is made, but if it was malicious trespass to personal property it should be five times the value. The trespass to real property, though intentional, was not regarded as malicious, but if one slandered or libelled another malice was implied. These examples are cited by way of general illustration. The criminal statutes were full of the most absurd distinctions, and they are yet to a material extent. The entire mass of criminal legislation is far behind the advance made in all other directions, and legislators seem blind to the progress made on all sides, and that the principles included in the criminal legislation are far behind and are not the ones on which the law should be based.

In some things in all of the states and in many things in some of the states material advancement has been made, and a dawn of the true requirements in criminal legislation is becoming visible. Committees from the legislature visit the prisons to examine them and report the results of what they find and conclude on; but generally they are persons with little or no experimental knowledge or education upon the subject of either criminals or prisons. Their visits are hurried and brief, and the whole acquisition of knowledge is of little or no practical value. The visit is expected at the prison, the best foot is forward for the reception, and the report, like the knowledge gained, is of no especial value as a basis for criminal legislation.

As a rule, boards of prison trustees, directors, inspectors, and supervising officers under various names, are selected on partisan grounds, from the general public, having no special knowledge as to criminals and prisons, and are seldom retained on change of party supremacy. There are some exceptions, but this action is that generally taken.

There can be no doubt that the entire course of legislative action on the subject, as a whole, is unwise and impractical. It ought to be abandoned and a correct course of action be adopted, based entirely upon the intendment of the fundamental law ; a code " founded on the principle of reformation." Legislation to that end would not be difficult or complicated. I can only briefly outline some of the things it evidently should include in a general way, or rather, indicate the spirit of the legislative action.

First, there should be a clear and distinct definition of what acts the law will regard as criminal, classified and named, and the immediate penalty should be, the commitment of the offender to the proper prison, male, female or juvenile. There should be no term fixed, unless a minimum term be fixed for each grade, within which the offender shall not be discharged ; and to remain until discharged by law. Beyond the minimum term (sooner than which there should be no discharge, unless innocence be shown) it should be indefinite and leave it dependent upon the condition of the criminal—his fitness to go at large and on what conditions—when he may do so, or whether he shall be continuously restrained. The character of the crime and the depravity shown in committing it, should determine the least period in the sentence for confinement, while all the highest grades should be for life. Such as wilful murder without palliation, rape, child stealing, arson, the use of explosives to destroy persons or property, whether any one be injured or not, wrecking of railroad trains, highway robbery, wilful perjury by which any innocent person is convicted of crime or their life is endangered, the wilful maiming of another without provocation by which they are crippled for life. These kinds of offences evidence a depravity and mental condition that precludes all hope of reformation, and the one who commits them should forfeit every right to personal liberty.

The state prison should consist of a succession of prisons, graded for the purpose intended, and consisting of not less than three—a receiving and reforming prison ; an intermediate restraining prison for the unreformable but not vicious class ;

and the incorrigible prison, for the hardened and irreclaimable. I shall speak of prisons separately, and notice them here only so far as is necessary to discuss the subject in hand. The sentence to prison should send the criminal to the receiving prison, there to remain unless, under the rules, he proves unreformable or irreclaimable, when he should be sent forward to either of the others.

A prison board should be provided for as a subordinate government agency, a municipal corporation, with powers of local legislation for the erection and repair of prisons ordered by the legislature, and for the government and management in prisons. Its action should be called for in report by the legislature at any time, and be subject to revision and modification, but should be authoritative until modified. It should not have power, like a city, to create any vested rights in its contracts or dealings to the injury of the interests of the state, but should have liberal powers in relation to providing for proper restraint, treatment, and disposition of convicts committed. It should have power to parol criminals and recommend to the pardoning power for pardon, under restrictions connected with a board of charities and correction. It should appoint the warden, physician, and chaplain of the prisons, and have supervisory control over all their appointees and assistants, with power to suspend or remove them for cause. The members should hold their office during competency and good behavior, but be removable by the governor or legislature for cause, on charges preferred by any responsible person, on trial and finding against them. The law should be plain, simple, direct, free from complications, and with a view to crystallize the subject matter under one competent management, ably officered, amply compensated, and protected from improper interference, so that a system may be established and maintained that will constantly tend to accomplish the end desired, to wit: the reformation of the reformable, the safe restraint of the unreformable, and a compensatory utility of all while under imprisonment. This cannot be done by any shifting or changeable policy, of either officials or plans. All promising plans should be tried, and all officials should become educated; and the only hope for good results is in stability of judicious management.

The code of procedure in criminal cases should be designed to screen the innocent, and hold the guilty when once charged with offence. A mass of chaff that now clogs the proceedings in court should be winnowed out, and many so-called safeguards, that oftener prove to be the reverse, and all technicalities, should be removed.

The acts complained of by government, in every charge, should be plainly and clearly stated, without technicalities or useless legal formalites, and they should come clearly within the line of the definition of the statutory offence complained of. If the defendant be plainly advised of what he is charged with, no want of formality should be permitted to hinder or obstruct the hearing. He should be permitted to make any statement of defence he may have in like manner, and always have the implied defence of "not guilty." He should be allowed to be a witness in his own behalf. No presumptions should be allowed against him only such as properly attend on and grow out of the evidence. The case should be fairly tried on its merits, freed from all useless technicalities, with an honest effort to get at the truth and clearly disclose if, in fact, the defendant be guilty or innocent; and the court should have power to pursue any line of inquiry that will show the existence of all the facts as they are; those in provocation or palliation of the act; those that show the capacity of the defendant to comprehend the force and consequences of the act, or the reverse; and disclose every material thing that will show the true relations existing between defendant and government, as to being a wilful and malicious offender, or an ignorant and not wilful one, or an accidental one. The agreement of two-thirds of the jurors should constitute a verdict.

If a defendant have incompetent counsel, the court should be required to see that such full and meritorious defence as he may have is laid before the court or jury; and that neither from his ignorance or poverty, or inability of his counsel, he is deprived of what honest defence he may have. All argument should be strictly confined to the allegations and the evidence, to the record as made in the case and the law applicable to it.

Before trial the defendant with his counsel should be afforded an interview with the court and prosecutor. They should inform him with what he is charged, and that inquiry by trial is about to be made to learn if the charge is true; and they should advise him fully as to the penalty. That it is the duty of the ministers of the law to ascertain if the charge be true, and if true he will be subject to the penalty. That the law protects him as well as every other person, and if the charge is not true, the law officers are as desirous that it shall be made to appear, as they are that it be shown he is guilty, if that be true. That he is not required to make any statement, but if he desires to make any he can do so. That they will use any facts he gives them as they would any other knowledge, to aid in discovering if the charge be true or false, and the opportunity is given to him to give any facts that may aid in that discovery.

The prosecutor should be sworn as the grand jurors are sworn; to prosecute no one from hatred, envy, malice, or ill will, nor for the mere purpose of securing a conviction because the defendant is charged, without respect to the real question of his guilt; nor will he leave any unprosecuted from fear, favor, affection, reward or the hope of any; but in all prosecutions he will honestly, fairly and to the best of his ability endeavor to discover and disclose the truth or falsity of the charge as made, to the end that the guilty may be convicted and the innocent be vindicated. It is too much the practice for prosecutors to forget that they represent the people, including the defendant, and to remember only that they are lawyers and must win their case against all odds. As lawyer and official they should exert themselves for a perfectly fair trial; for they " win their case " when by that course an honest and just verdict is obtained, whether the charge be sustained or disproved.

One of the absurdities and barbarisms of the statutes as now enforced—as it has always seemed to me—is the distinction between proceedings before the grand and petit juries in most respects; and also between the oath and the action of the grand jury. The grand jury is intended to be a bulwark between the state and abuse of the criminal law by any one. It is also a wall of protection for all persons against a malicious use of the criminal law to persecute

others. No person charged with offence has any voice in
the selection of the jurors. They constitute an independent
body for the sole purpose of inquiry. They are "the grand
inquest," unhampered by rules or technicalities in their
search as to the truth or falsity of charges. They are sworn
to well and diligently inquire into such matters as may come
before them or be given them in charge by the court; and
make a true presentment in writing of their findings to the
court. That neither hatred, envy, malice, or ill will on the one
hand, nor fear, favor, affection, or reward, or the hope of it, on
the other, shall cause them to make a presentment against any
one or neglect to present any one; and in all they do present
they will present the truth, the whole truth and nothing but
the truth. They have the prosecutor for a legal adviser if they
wish his advice. They may ask the court for any instructions
as to their duties and how to discharge them. They may act
exclusively on their own judgment. They sit with closed
doors, make their inquiries secretly, and are sworn to keep
secret whatever transpires before them.

Now what are their *duties* under this oath and the legal
obligations of their office? It is, to diligently inquire as to the
truth of any matter laid before them, as to violations of
the criminal statutes; and to do this the entire power of the
state is at their command and service. But what is the *practice?* Why, to only half inquire. To examine only such
witnesses as those making the charge bring forward. When
they have been heard, if the jury thinks a probable case is
made it makes a presentment under oath that the accused
committed the crime. The person charged knows nothing of
the charge or inquiry in some cases. If his side had been
"diligently" inquired into, possibly no presentment would
have been made. In the very necessity of the case the jury
do not know if they have presented the whole truth. It will
not do to say that only the state's evidence was given them in
charge, for that is not true, and it defeats the protection intended and aids in persecution if intended. It will not do to
say such has always been the practice, for it is a wrong practice and should be discontinued. The first thing given in
charge was an accusation of crime against some person. As

to that, they are to inquire and ascertain the truth and the whole truth, sift out from everything before them all but the truth. That they are to present. How can that be done with inquiry as to only one side? And how does the grand inquest aid to prevent persecution if persons making accusations are alone to have a hearing?

When the presentment based on half inquiry is made, and which a majority of the jury can do in some states, the accused is taken into custody and another inquiry is made openly in court before another jury, in which full and diligent inquiry is made as to both sides; but that jury cannot convict on a probability; it must find the presentment to be true beyond all reasonable doubt, and the full jury must agree.

It is hardly possible to escape the impression of a gross inconsistency in this kind of proceeding as a means of securing justice to either the state or the accused. Let us suppose a change made in the law to this effect: As soon as a charge is laid before the prosecutor or the grand jury on which inquiry must be made, or in cases of suspicion where inquiry is made, as soon as the jury finds enough facts to convince it that full inquiry should be made as to any particular person, that the accused in the one case or the suspected in the other, is taken into custody and bailed, if a bailable offence, or held until inquiry can be made. He is informed of the charge or suspicion. The grand jury are to make diligent inquiry and present the truth as now, and the inquiry is to be to learn the whole truth, and they are to differ from a petit jury only in this: they need not be convinced beyond doubt, but may present the facts as they believe them to be, although every avenue inconsistent with innocence .may not be closed; although further time and inquiry may disclose facts not now apparent, justifying other conclusions. They are not bound and held by the formalities and technicalities of a trial in court and may hear and consider anything that tends to elicit the truth—statements that could not go before a petit jury—questions that could not be asked there. If they believe the accused guilty, and find what they believe to be evidence admissible in court sufficient to prove guilt, then make the presentment. In such an inquiry (at such stage of the inquiry as they deem best) they should give the accused a chance to be heard, and inquire into such accessible sources of information as he may furnish. In a word, seek to discover the whole truth. They are not limited or restrained or hampered, and have every advantage to secure evidence to show every material fact, and to protect themselves against imposition, unreasonable delay and useless expense. No technicalities as to questions, evidence, hearsay, or procedure, limit the inquiry. On such an inquiry no injustice could be done to any one. Without such inquiry great injustice may be done and is now often done. Where the accused cannot be arrested the inquest can go on ; but the jury should inquire as to his innocence as well as to his guilt, as far as any facts can be made to appear by diligent inquiry, and the presentment should show if arrest has been made or not. Such a proceeding could be rightly called " the grand inquest ;" but as now conducted it is anything but grand. In inquiry proceeding on suspicion, it can be secret until it is deemed enough is disclosed to arrest the accused, and he can then be held until the inquiry is ended. When a presentment comes before a petit jury, the accused having been arrested, there should be no useless technicalities to obstruct or hinder diligent inquiry as to the exact truth of the presentment. The grand jury inquires as to crime and who committed it. The petit jury formally tries the particular person on the specific charge presented. One is unlimited, the other limited. If the accused voluntarily absents himself, the hearing should go on as if he were present. The prosecutor and court should see to it that all of the evidence is presented, that the truth may be known. If there be a conviction the court should enter judgment and the convict be sent to prison whenever re-arrested. Having had his day in court and waived every advantage of being present, he should be precluded as he would be had he been present. The constitution could be readily amended so as to admit of these modifications where needed, and some of them could be made without such amendment.

With these suggestions—perhaps only hints, for they can hardly be called more—as to modifications in regard to criminal legislation, I desire to present some other views that are germane to the subject matter. The sole end and aim of the law is, to accomplish justice. If any particular statute alone, or any part of the law in combination with other parts so operates as to create antagonisms which defeat that aim, it is bad legislation and should be modified or repealed. The laws should be framed and so enforced as to command the confidence and respect of the people. Every statute should be so framed that the spirit of justice will be visible when it is enforced. No bill for an act should pass the legislature until its provisions are so formulated as to meet not only this requirement as to its own operations, but it should be ascertained how it will affect or be affected by other laws already in force, and what will be the effect of antagonism or modifications in any and all forms that may arise. Especially should inquiry be made as to the necessity for and the utility of the proposed act. If decided on, then it should be so framed as to leave no doubt as to the legislative intention, and that the end of the law—the accomplishment of justice—will be apparent in its operation.

In relation to criminal law, no respect can be felt for statutes that, like the hypocrite who, "with one hand puts a penny in the urn of poverty and with the other takes a shilling out," in one set of provisions provide for and sanction the unlimited procreation of criminal mentalities, and in another set of provisions punish the victims as offenders, support them by the labors of honest people, and try to reform them and turn them loose again. It is absurd to tax people to build and maintain prisons and reformatories, and then enact laws that permit of the certain procreation of more people than will keep them full. Yet that is exactly what the legislation now in force accomplishes. In the first place, no restraint or limitations are provided in relation to marriage among those who are totally unfit for that relation. Both state and church take part in uniting people in marriage without inquiry, and the officials in both know that, the issue in many cases must be of a vicious character, either pauper, or criminal, or incurably diseased. The results are, a constant procession of criminals and sinners starting at the cradles and moving into the public institutions, leaving more or less evil influences along the way. The resources of the state are heavily taxed to support, and in fruitless efforts to reform, what it has aided to deform; and the church is calling for aid on all hands to support it while it seeks to make Christians out of those it has aided in making sinners. This subject should receive legislative attention, on the lines suggested in the chapter on marriage. As now operative the law does constant violence to "the principle of reformation."

Another consideration relates to the palatial provisions for the unfortunate classes. The buildings prepared for the insane cost from ten to twelve hundred dollars for each patient it is intended to accommodate. That is equal to the cost of a good residence for a fair-sized family. With the exception of a few, the majority of the inmates come from among the classes of people that have never known anything of luxuries or more than the most common provisions; while no inconsiderable number are from the pauper and criminal classes. Very few of them are ever really cured. A strong mind occasionally may become unbalanced and be restored. Many are sent out as cured, but while they may be sane they are not cured and are liable to relapse at any time. To go back to a home and provisions very far below the level of the asylum—some to a pauper's fare—and become the progenitors of offspring, is inimical to their own and the public good; and as business—conducted by government—it is the exact policy of the one who, on the pretence of aiding charity, robs the poor.

The prevailing methods operate to create inordinate expense to care for and reform the evil, worthless and unbalanced classes, while constantly increasing their numbers. It is much like the government in need of a navy, pursuing the following policy: While it has unlimited supplies of sound, suitable timber, inexhaustible mines of mineral, and abundant sources of the best supplies of every kind, it converts it into money, and then goes along its coasts, digs up the wrecks and buried hulks of ships, and uses their decayed and deteriorated material to build naval ships with. It employs and pays the best talent and ability to prepare yards, machinery and docks to build the vessels and equip them, and then turns the guns upon its own towns and cities and bombards the property of their occupants. The government needs a sound, sane and healthy population. It has the best of stock from which to produce it. Instead, it permits and encourages the production of the most worthless at home, and opens its ports to unlimited immigration of the same kind from abroad. It squanders immense sums for schools, asylums, almshouses, reformatories, orphans' and foundlings' homes, homes for abandoned women, feeble-minded children, industrial schools for incorrigible youths, houses of refuge, and other institutions, provides them with the highest ability and skill for managers, physicians and other officials, furnishes them luxuriously to receive, care for, treat, educate and reform these classes, taxing the sound and healthy people to pay the expense. It then turns the worthless classes loose to become members of society, electors, and political factors in means for government, and to contaminate and taint more or less, morally and physically, those they meet, and to become the progenitors of others. That is, they try to make sound persons of those already wrecked and decayed at the expense of sound people, and then use them to produce more unsound ones; exactly like selling the sound material and using the navy made of wrecks with the money, in bombarding the coasts that need protection.

While these classes should be properly provided for, it should be in an entirely different way from the one now followed. Architectural skill of the highest order designs and erects palatial buildings. Landscape gardeners design the most beautiful grounds; professional florists, with elaborate hot-houses and conservatories and unstinted means, cultivate as if for some royal family; elegantly furnished apartments, with every modern convenience, as if for aristocratic guests of the finest hotel, are provided for officials and employés in the provisions for many institutions. When we approach and enter one of these institutions we are impressed as we might be on entering the residence of some nobleman or prince. Not one of the inmates—from the highest official to the weakest patient—has ever lived with any such surroundings of their own. The wards of the state are, nearly all of them, from among the plain and poorer classes of the people. The cost and expense of all of it is paid from the taxes levied on the labor of the country—for on that it all falls in the end. The sound, healthy,

industrious and moral, who live plain, work hard, know little
of luxury and many know nothing of it, pay to help support
all this extravagance for those who are unsound and diseased;
some are immoral or criminal; some are idiotic, and scarcely
one is capable of being made so they can contribute to the
expense of, or in any way help to uphold government, or, un-
aided, even provide for themselves. Not twenty per cent. of
them are ever made fit for the duties of citizenship and the responsibilities of life. It is sentimental fallacy substituted for
philosophical reason that has established such conditions and
practice. It is a false use of the power of legislation to enact
laws to carry out such systems. One hundredth part of the
effort and expense now used, if used in wise efforts to prevent
the production of these classes, would effect more in one
decade in reducing the number, than can be fitted for the responsible duties of life in these institutions in a century. Reasonable and proper provisions should be made for these classes,
but the senseless extravagance that has been indulged in
should cease.

In contrast with this extravagance on one hand, there is an
erroneous idea prevailing on the other, in some cases, that
public parsimony is public economy. This is notably exhibited in providing officials for prison affairs. The legislature
seems to provide as if competent men will be patriotic enough
to give their best energies to public use without compensation
—finding that in the honor of the position. The truth is, that
the man of honor with the necessary ability, is either busily
engaged with affairs of his own and has no spare time to give
away, or if he has no business and is independent, he is not willing to surrender his personal comfort and domestic pleasures,
to assume the specially onerous duties involved in an efficient
and honest supervision of prisons and criminals. The occupants for such positions must be looked for among the class
of persons who are willing to accept compensation, who are
worth it, and who will devote their best efforts to the duties
required, for a sufficent compensation. The compensation
should be sufficient to command the very best. A man who
has never been able to earn and lay up something, will often
seek a salaried office far above his abilities to manage properly,

and all intermediate positions are eagerly sought by impecu-
nious candidates. The offices are like a baited trap set by law
and the strife commences to see who can get the bait and miss
the trap; the candidates and their friends proceed to so manage
voters—with little scruple as to means—as in their opinions
will secure the office. Promises, misrepresentations, bribes,
and all the means used in "machine politics" are brought to
bear. The shrewdest, and not the best always, gets the bait
and leaves the others in the trap. Prisons especially, should
be put entirely beyond the reach of this influence. The state
is able and should provide all that is required to preserve the
public peace and order by removing and restraining all disturbing elements. The means that will do it the most certainly
and effectually, and show as much favor to offenders as that
kind of means will permit, is the cheapest and most economical, no matter what it costs. There should be no emoluments
or perquisites attached to any position. The compensation
should be fixed by law, the incumbent be required to render
every service demanded by the place, and be held to strict ac-
countability. All perquisites, if any are provided for, should
go to the state toward paying expenses. The compensation
should be liberal enough to justify such ability as is desired in
accepting it, and devoting the proper time and attention to
the duties; and all legislation providing for officials and employés should be based on the principles here presented. Men
who *want* official position want it in order to make something
out of it; either money, or as a stepping-stone to something
higher, and opening better opportunities to make money. It
is not patriotism or benevolence that moves them as a whole.
There are some exceptions, but they are not likely to be found
among those needed as officials in connection with criminals
and prisons. No official position in connection with either
has anything in it likely to add to one's comfort or pleasure,
and therefore, they will not be sought by the order of ability
that can best fill them, but by those I have named. Hence,
such compensation should be fixed and qualifications required,
as will induce the best to accept the place, and by having the
best the state's interests will be best served.

In all legislation relating to criminals and prisons the legislature should look at the subject as a matter of *business* in government, entirely. The first step in any just system must be based on the idea—the necessity—of protection to those who would preserve the public order, and that order must conform to a practical and consistent standard of right and wrong, temporary though it may be. It should be made to govern men as we find them, regardless of what they may believe as to the past or desire or hope as to the future. That is, it must be a determinate one to which individuals must conform, whatever their individual opinions or hopes may be.

Under existing conditions we may be justified in asserting that, whatever will give the greatest latitude to individuals consistent with public order, and avoid infringement upon others, is right. That which, in the acts of individuals, infringes upon others or tends to disorder, is wrong.

Whatever tends to elevate and refine, intellectually and socially, is right. That which tends to degrade and make coarse and ignorant, is wrong.

Whatever tends to physical and mental improvement and perfection, is right. That which tends to physical and mental disease and deterioration, is wrong.

In propositions for details under these principles the opinion of the majority expressed according to the forms prescribed by law, must be authoritative. We may look to reason and experience for a guide in maintaining these propositions, and in fixing the limits upon the statute books, so far as statutory law can be made operative. The theory is, to so provide as to encourage right and prohibit wrong. Prohibition does not follow any punishment inflicted by the state to any encouraging extent. Legislation should repel the idea of punishment by the state, and regard it only as an element of discipline in the prison. It should repel the idea of humiliating and degrading the convict by the state. That belongs with punishment as an element of prison discipline. It should exclude all sentimentality and provide for the public safety and welfare as the highest order of business, in government. The penalties fixed by the statute should not be for punishment, but as a *condition* following the forfeiture of civil rights as a result from crime; which condition the convict voluntarily places himself

in. Provisions for punishment should come through regulations of the prison board, for discipline, and among the means
for reformation. Legislation should provide for preventing
the infliction of cruel and unusual punishments in the prisons ;
but nothing can be more mischievous and absurd than the
state's attempting by law to inflict punishment. It can provide for deprivation of liberty and property, as forfeitures that
will follow prohibited or forbidden acts, but it does not operate as punishment any more than any other loss from breach
of contract. It is a misuse of the word to talk about punishment by the state. That burden upon and absurdity in legislation should be removed.

Legislation should provide for a State Board of Charities
and Correction. (This has been done by several of the states,
but they need enlarged powers.) It should have the powers of
a court. It should be composed of the highest obtainable
ability. It should be so constituted as to be non-partisan and
non-sectarian, and the compensation sufficient to justify able
persons to devote the requisite time to the duties. The tenure
should be long enough to ensure efficiency and be made as
permanent as possible. The members should be removed only
for incompetency, inefficiency and malfeasance. It should
have general supervision over all charitable and reformatory
institutions in the state, public and private, with power as a
court to make and enforce necessary orders to secure obedience
to the law. It should make frequent visits and inspection of
all public institutions; examine into all contracts made for
supplies and the manner in which they are executed; how
supplies are delivered, cared for, distributed and disposed of;
all receipts and expenditures; how accounts and records are
kept; how inmates are cared for and treated and how employés perform their duties. It should prosecute for removal
any incompetent official, and for removal and punishment any
who are guilty of neglect of duty or malfeasance in office. In
connection with the governor it should constitute a Board of
Pardons, and in connection with the Prison Board, a Board of
Parole for convicts. It should examine all rules made for
government of institutions and have authority to modify and
amend them ; except, that it should not have power to control

the action of the Prison Board, or modify or change its rules, only, when sitting as a court it judicially finds such change necessary on the ground of public policy. But it should at any time recommend such change as it may deem advisable. On its recommendation, the governor should be required to suspend until tried, any official connected with any institution, and with the board appoint some other to act until the vacancy be filled with the old or a new incumbent. It should have power to visit and inspect private charities, when, in its opinion, such action is needed, or on complaint made by any competent person ; and when necessary, to cause issues to be made and tried, as to any institution, and make orders to carry out the true intent, meaning and object of the law relating to the institutions and their inmates. Appeals by writ of error should be allowed from its judicial action to the supreme court. In all cases, except where punishment for corruption in office is contemplated, it should proceed summarily, on notice to persons to be affected. In cases where parties would be entitled to trial by jury, it should certify the case to some court having general jurisdiction, and see that the case is prosecuted. With such a body, efficient and economical management would be likely to characterize the institutions, and the best results be reached.

The Bertillon System for the identification of convicts has been sufficiently tested to establish it as of great value, and legislation for its adoption should be made efficient. When legislation shall have defined public offences, provided a code of procedure excluding technicality, and framed to elicit the truth as completely as possible, provided for the commitment of convicts without limit as to time, and the term dependent entirely on their becoming fit to be trusted at large, providing a progressive system of prisons, a permanent and competent prison board with authority to provide for prison management and conduct, with proper limits and restraint on that authority, but leaving details to it, and for a State Board of Charities and Correction with proper supervisory power, and finally, for a system of identification of convicts, it will have done all that is possible. Time and experience, as shown in the reports of officials, will indicate the necessary modifications and changes requiring further legislative action. It is impracticable for legislation to provide for, carry into practice or enforce the details necessary. Any attempt to do so must result in iron-clad, inelastic provisions, that cannot be adapted to the ever changing conditions and constantly arising emergencies, and they would defeat the very ends intended to be served. That difficulty now hampers reformatories already on trial.

There is another matter that has strongly impressed itself on me, and I will refer to it. The matter of supplies and dis-position of prison products should be a distinct department, and be established under direction of the prison board, or by direct legislation. The requisition for supplies should be made by the prison authorities—the warden or whoever may be designated as the proper party—and the agency established for that purpose should furnish them. The persons who manage the prisons should never be burdened with or be called upon to go into the markets to contract for and furnish sup-plies or dispose of products. It would be equally inconsistent as it would be with an army regulation requiring the major general of a department to furnish all supplies and dispose of all property to be sold. The same agency should dispose of all prison products. They should be turned over to that agency when ready for market, (all such as are made for the state, I mean), and the warden have nothing to do with their disposition. In this way the agency can be placed under safe supervision, and the most advantageous terms can be secured; while the prison officials will be left free to devote exclusive attention to the work in their charge, which is of a character as inconsistent with the duties of such an agency, as that of a general in command of a department is inconsistent with that of a quartermaster. In my judgment, proper legislation should be had in relation to this matter, and so further serve the interests of the state to the best advantage.

CHAPTER XI.

CONVICTS AND GOVERNMENT.

THE convicts for crime come from every social level. Representatives of every grade of intelligence are found among them. They include persons without one redeeming trait of character, those with "a single virtue linked to a thousand crimes," and those with many virtues linked to a single crime. Among them are found the most ignorant and the most brutal of human beings; educated and intelligent persons with a brutal nature; persons without education that are full of kindness and good humor, subject to one single vicious impulse; those with the external display of kindness and courtesy, but with a soul full of malice and devoid of pity; those with an irritable nervousness, that are lost to reason when greatly aggravated, and they rush blindly toward the gratification of the leading impulse without reflection, or thought, or intention, guided by mere animal instinct inflamed by overpowering passion; those with no criminal mentality, but subject to mental influences that compel them to reason in the direction of what they do, and to believe they have the right to do it, that everything that forbids it is wrong, and it is a right they have to defeat the wrong in any way they can. There are those with no actual vicious tendencies who lack moral perception and are ignorant, and through both causes become offenders. There are those who are so constituted that they are as if insane; cannot control their impulses and with full knowledge yield to them. I may forcibly illustrate this by the statement of a fact. A noted professor lectured on phrenology before a large and intelligent audience in one of our largest cities. He permitted himself to be blindfolded, and then, well known persons—strangers to him—were selected from the audience for him to examine while blindfolded, that they might judge of the truth of his theory. After some examinations had been concluded, a fine, intelligent looking, well-dressed man, followed closely by another, walked upon the platform and said, " I have no faith in your science, but I would like to have you examine me, and if you can tell the truth about me I shall become a convert. I wish you to tell all you think you find developed." The professor proceeded and disclosed a finely developed brain as far as he went. He assumed from appearances that the subject was educated; if so, he possessed rare ability; and he gave some specific instances of development and combinations, but did not go into much detail. When through, the gentleman said, " Have you told all you can find there? If not, tell all you find. I want to know it all as far as you can discover." The professor said, " No. I can tell more. If you desire me to tell more thus publicly I can tell it," and he seemed somewhat excited. The gentleman said, " Go on, tell all you think is shown." The professor said, " I know nothing about you, sir. I know what your brain development shows. You may be an honest, upright man, but your brain combinations show you to be instinctively a thief and with the ability to make a very successful one." Without waiting for more the gentleman arose and said, " I am converted. That is just what I am. I am well born and bred and have ample means. I am well educated. I can gratify every desire in every way; but I can no more avoid stealing than I can breathing. It makes no difference what it may be—a pair of baby's shoes, a diamond, or anything else that can be taken—I must take it if the chance occurs, and I have no power to resist the impulse. I am well connected and my family is well known. This man" (pointing to the one who had followed him) "is a guardian and I am never out of sight of one, and never have been since it became settled that I am thus affected. I am not known to any one here, but this is the truth, and I now believe that phrenology has a scientific basis." And he left the platform.

There are untold thousands of not only these so-called kleptomaniacs, but those subject to irresistible impulses in other directions: notably a desire to fire buildings, destroy property, and take life. I was close by an exhibition of the murderous impulse on one occasion. The victim of the impulse, in the presence of several, was sitting on a table in a public room. A man came in whom he knew well and with whom he was on friendly terms. He drew a pistol and said, " Jake, I have a notion to shoot you." The other, having no idea he meant it, said, " What do you want to shoot me for?" He went on doing the errand he came for and laughingly said, " You wouldn't kill a fly." The other said, " I'll give you one any how," and he fired, killing the man. He left the table, backed to the door, pointing his pistol at the others who started toward him, and threatening to shoot, and escaped up an alley. It all transpired in two or three miuntes, and there was nothing at any time to give rise to anything that could in any way lead to such an act except a mere insane impulse to take life. The murderer bore an unsavory reputation, but no one had any idea of any disposition in him to murder.

There are others who have no criminal tendencies, but will stop at nothing in efforts to have revenge for some real or fancied injury; and yet are entirely free from criminal impulse in all other directions. Others have no tendency to crime but have a desire for mischief; and when started on some mischievousness, perhaps comparatively innocent, with no intent to do real harm, it seems to rouse and feed a desire—until then latent—to go further; and a disposition to destroy becomes active. Gratification in some cases seems to beget a frenzy that drives them to extreme acts, with no power to resist. Others become involuntary criminals; opening a door without any evil intention and in time finding it impossible to close it—such as using a small portion of money intrusted to their care temporarily, feeling sure of the ability and with the intention of replacing it, but from some cause being unable, resort to temporary concealment until they can replace it. Being still unable, they are detected with only the one misstep. Others go on taking more, still intending to make it good; but become unable to do so, abscond and so become fugitives. The door once open, with dishonor pursuing, with no natural criminal tendencies, from necessity they become criminals, seeing no other way open to live. Others in places of trust, with no tendencies to crime, are persuaded to accommodate friends with temporary loans from moneys in their care, which are not repaid and they are found in default and convicted of embezzlement. Still others in like position, driven by great and pressing want—the necessities of a sick family, perhaps—take a little, intending to replace it before it can be missed, open a door that growing necessities prevent them from closing until detection ensues; and while not criminals they become convicts as embezzlers. Others, again, are easily misled; are deceived and used by sharpers as tools; and left in such a position as to become liable to charge and conviction, when they are free from any voluntary intention to commit crime. Others become involuntary criminals by doing something they thought they had a right to do and overstep the legal limits, which they would not have done had they known it was illegal. Still others are made criminals by education and environment, with no natural tendency to crime. There is a very large number who are either born with a criminal mentality, or fall into channels when young that create one, and their normal condition is that of offenders and their practices consist in the commission of crimes. Some progress to a certain limit within the line of petty offenses and never beyond. Others cross that line and stop at the lower grade of felonies. Others still, progress throughout the scale to the highest order of offences, and when they start in to commit a lesser crime expect to commit murder, if necessary, to escape detection or capture. Others, again, start high and never descend to lesser offences, and follow it with success and profit.

There are more criminals outside the world of convicts than there are in it, many times over; and in both worlds may be found every grade of mentality, temper and disposition that can be found throughout society. Among the convicts are some entirely innocent persons; others who ought not to have been convicted though in the position of offenders; and when we come to take a prison full of convicts, what to do with them to do justice to each one and to the public, becomes a problem that requires a Divine mind to solve. Finite man can only partially solve it, and bring to bear his best judgment in dealing with such results as he can comprehend.

There is something unexplainable about the impressions

made upon the public mind by the commission of different kinds of crime. There is a vindictiveness and bitterness that knows no kind of softening against horse-stealing. Not even the ravisher of women is regarded with such contempt and feelings for revenge as is the horse-thief. The successful purloiner of many thousands and the successful forger for large sums, is regarded by many with a feeling akin to admiration; while the chicken-thief, the hog-thief, and the pickpocket creates a feeling that he ought to be tortured and then killed to get rid of him. The bank president and cashier who deliberately wreck a bank and knowingly swindle depositors and others out of thousands, are rarely looked upon with vindictiveness, and not unfrequently find many who are sorry for them; while the fire-bug, the robber or the burglar who may do injury to but a small amount, stimulates a feeling in favor of calling Judge Lynch to the bench and removing the offender under his order.

When a person is charged with crime there is a disposition to look for the marks of a criminal in his appearance and in all he does and says; everything is seen through the medium of suspicion and construed on the theory of guilt. None ever think of looking for signs of integrity or innocence in his appearance and actions, and the victim lies under this incubus if innocent, from his arrest until he lands in prison if convicted—to which result the mental condition of the public strongly aids.

Whatever may be the character of the convict, when once in prison he becomes the ward, servant and apprentice of the state, as I have sought to show in the chapter on government and the criminal; and these certain relations that grow out of the conditions bring into operation natural forces that should be recognized and regarded. Under the law in most of the states the convict is subjected to a specific penalty—committed for a definite term—and he is considered as under the ban of the state until the penalty has been suffered, when he will be released, whether he is better or worse for the state's action. Certain limitations, restrictions, and presumptions in his favor, provided for by law, put both the convict and his keepers in a position that antagonizes the operation of the natural forces arising from the conditions, and in effect hinders, or entirely prevents the accomplishment of the results. contemplated in the law. In the light of some of the principles asserted in the foregoing chapters I desire to look at these relations.

When an offence is committed the prevailing idea is to catch the offender and punish him. That is an erroneous perception of the relations between the offender and the public. The true idea is—and should be understood so—to remove the offender from society because he is a disturbing element. When he is arrested the state has him in custody for that reason and no other; and in the discharge of one of the duties and purposes of government—that of protecting persons and property by preserving public order—it arrests and holds him. The implied contract between every responsible person and the state—and between the parent or guardian of every irresponsible person and the state—is, that the person shall keep the peace and bear a portion of the expense of government, in return for personal liberty and protection for person and property in the enjoyment of that liberty. The implied contract between society and government is, that every irresponsible person shall have a guardian who will be a competent party to the contract. When the person breaks the peace he violates the contract, forfeits the right to liberty, and endangers the persons in society, and property, and government must perform its contract with them by depriving the offender of his liberty, and putting it out of his power to make further breach of his contract. Should government not do so, itself would be guilty of a breach of contract with every person who could be unfavorably affected by the act of the offender. This includes every relation between the inhabitant and government up to this point, in this connection.

In performance of its obligation, government seizes the offender, deprives him of the liberty he has voluntarily forfeited, fastens the offence on him by trial and judgment, and new relations at once come into existence, and new forces begin to operate. The stability and well-being of society are wholly dependent on the practical intelligence and moral perception and conduct of its members. Here is one who, no matter what his intelligence and moral perceptions are, has so used his opportunities as to end in conduct that is not moral, and he has been removed from society. But one of two things can be rightly done with him : either extirpate him, or make him of use to the state for the benefit of the public he has injured, and keep him from doing more harm. The right of the government to extirpate him is a questionable right. It has established or permitted the social conditions under which he came here and reached his present status, and so has sanctioned his coming. It took the chances as to what he would be, and natural forces growing out of the conditions have made the implied contract between him and government. He has broken the contract, but that hardly authorizes government to destroy him. If government has that right, it is a right without limit and extends with equal force to every relation that can produce a dangerous or disturbing element. If government can now seize and destroy him because he breaks the peace by committing murder, it can seize and destroy any one who must—in the nature of things—become a disturber of the peace. If it may seize, search, examine and try one on a charge of crime, put him away and keep him, or take his life, much more may it seize, search, examine, try, and put away one who may become the progenitor of a race of criminals, or of other deformities, to become a public burden, and in any manner put it out of their power to become not only perpetual disturbers of the peace, but vicious contaminators of society, and breeders of ignorance, of immoral perception and immoral conduct, instead of practical intelligence, with moral perception and conduct. When government assumes the right to take the life of offenders in order to keep and perform its contract with the people to preserve the peace, and protect each in liberty of person and rights of property, then, logically and rightly, the power extends to the full limit, and it becomes the duty of government to prevent the coming and maturing of criminal mentalities, in all cases where it can and probably will result from existing conditions and customs. It is a glaring inconsistency to uphold customs that produce criminals certainly, to provide for them until they commit crime in obedience to natural and hereditary impulse, and then deprive them of life. But if government exerts itself to prevent such customs, then it may con-*

sistently take life when a criminal mentality comes in spite of
government's prohibitions.   Therefore, I repeat that, under
the customs now upheld by government, it is questionable if it
has the right to take life.   See the chapters on mentality and
marriage.

Assuming that extirpation is not to follow judgment, it becomes the duty of government to make careful examination
and ascertain what it has seized and removed from society.   It
can take no step in advance of this one without plunging into
false positions and producing conditions that are inimical to
true relations between it and the convict; for its future relations, if justice is to be considered, if "the principle of reformation " is to be the rule of action as is required by the constitutional mandate — will be such that government must know
what kind of a subject it has got to deal with.   What is the
mental timbre as well as caliber of the convict in all ways;
what has been the education and environment that has made
it what it is ; to what extent it is impressible and what means
will best and soonest impress it ; to what extent is reformation
possible or probable, and what environment and daily usages
will soonest effect reform?   Examination to discover as much
of this as possible should be made and reasonable time be
given to it—a day, a week, a month, as may be necessary ;
and by any and all methods that may be available.

The convict now becomes the apprentice as well as the ward
of government.   The obligations of both guardian and master
attach to the state, and those of servant and ward attach to
the convict.   While the state in discharge of its duties as
guardian cares for his bodily comfort and shelter and protects
him, as his master it tries to teach him how to become a true
and orderly citizen as well as a useful and practical artisan.
While it gives him the best of hygiene for his corporal well-being,
it makes the best use it can of mental pathology, and tries to
create and establish a well-balanced mentality with clear moral
perceptions and good impulses.

If government can succeed in this—if it can make the convict clearly comprehend the relations between government and
the citizen, and understand the terms of his contract with
government, and endow him with a will and a firmness to per-

form it on his part, a new relation obtains. It is that of government and the reformed convict, and it is the duty of government to restore him to liberty, and make some provision for him to start on a career of self-support. But having broken the contract once, government may attach conditions to his restoration to liberty, such as it thinks will best hold him to the observance of the contract. These it may gradually remove; or if he lapses into wrong again, remove him and send him forward among the unreformables.

As a part of every prison system there should be provisions made for aiding discharged convicts to get started in a way to live; perhaps by wages after reformed for a period before discharge and then assistance to employment outside for a period, or in some other way. It is as clearly the duty of the state to provide for a convict it discharges, as it is to provide for those it imprisons. It is sending him out on trial. It has held him as a disturbing element and left him no chance to provide for himself. It should so arrange that when it believes its ward can be trusted at large, he can have some means with which to begin the new struggle for life, when he has none of his own. There is an argument made that, the convict while in custody can ask nothing at the hands of the state except the bare necessaries of life. That he has the same opportunities as the rest of the people. That only honesty, industry and close economy, if he be poor, will enable him to live and give him the law's protection. Those who do that are the ones who must contribute to the support of government and to the support of those who do not do it. If one sees proper to be idle, unthrifty and dishonest, he can have no right to demand anything from those who are not so. If unfortunate in any way, either from lack of ability, physical or mental, to make a living, he can avoid crime, and in that case the public must support him. But if he commits crime he should forfeit all rights, be made to labor for his own support and for that of his class, and fare no better than is necessary to give him health and strength to work. That it is gross injustice to tax honest labor to support rogues either any better than the commonest of honest laborers live, or at all in idleness; and it has reason in it.

It requires a liberal stretch of philanthropy to find warrant for taking money from honest labor to make dishonest idlers comfortable; teach them trades; furnish them books, papers and teachers; find them labor and amusements; and then give them means to start in life after doing all this, be it little or much; and the only reason for it all, because they are dangerous to the honest laborer and his property. In fact, there is no philanthropy in it at all. But under human imperfections in social conditions, as created or permitted by law, many become convicts who are actual offenders, but objects of pity as being more unfortunate than wilful. Others are innocent of crime and the victims of injustice from circumstances they could not control. These it is right to care for and aid. But the deliberate and wilful offender, with intelligence enough to know what he does, should forfeit all rights, even of a return to society on any conditions, and be used to earn what he can be made to in order to help support his class in prison. However, having been confined and supported by taxes levied on the orderly, if he is found fit to go back to liberty, public policy, regardless of the matter of individual right, dictates that some aid should be given in some form by the government; and arrangements should be made as a provision in the prison system, to aid liberated convicts to employment and temporary means to live.

In treating of punishment and prisons I shall have more to offer on the subject of convicts; in which I shall make further application of the principles laid down in the preceding chapters.

CHAPTER XII.

STRICTLY speaking, punishment is pain, inflicted as a penalty for the commission of a wrong. The object is, to deter the offender from a repetition of offence, and if publicly inflicted to deter others who might be inclined to do wrong. It is on this theory that the state through its criminal statutes undertakes to inflict punishment, and so effect reformation in those criminally inclined. That punishment by the state is impractical and will not reform, but rather, closes the door to reform, under the provisions now largely existing both as to criminal procedure and determinate sentences, I think I will be able to demonstrate. Then I will try to show how and when punishment can be practically resorted to and for what ends.

Going back to the beginning, in order that we may have a clear comprehension we must bring forward a few postulates from the principles already laid down.

Opinion is a temporary conclusion formed as to something brought within the line of our observation. When we have satisfactory evidence to sustain that opinion it becomes belief. Our opinions and beliefs depend upon our perceptions and they depend on our mentality and environment. No man can act any further than he can see—perceive—and his opinions and beliefs as to right and wrong will be as his perceptions are. A man's actions will be prompted by impulses begotten of his opinions. "What a man loves that he wills to do," says Swedenborg. We cannot reform everybody, and the rich and wise will rule the poor and ignorant, while the poor and ignorant will envy or hate the rich and wise. Ignorance and wealth we find united, as well as wisdom and poverty. Keeping ignorant wealth instead of intelligent poverty in the ascendency as consistent with morals, justice and public good, is maintained by society, while it is inconsistent with all of them.

The prevailing theory is, that punishment must be based on the idea of, and be inflicted with a view to, moral reformation; and it presents the question—can any system of punishment for public wrongs be conceived or established on any such basis? The standards of right and wrong being arbitrary and temporary presents the first difficulty. A portion of community erect conscience as a standard and rely upon it as a supernatural perception in each person. It has no influence on such as do not believe it, because they do not perceive the facts that lead to it. The greater number neither recognize nor adhere to this supernatural standard. We are forced back continually upon the truth that, a man's opinions will govern his actions, and his opinions depend on his mentality as made by congenital organization and subsequent impressions.

Keeping before us the social conditions of men as they are, the necessity for public order, the fact that no two opinions can be exactly alike, and the opinion of each is dependent on his mentality, a proposition to effect reform by a fixed system of punishment is an absurdity. The main thing presented by punishment is fear. The design is, to make the delinquent afraid of punishment—not afraid to offend. It is a fact that, fear will not operate as a restraint unless the danger feared is present or palpably close, and certain. Indirectly, statutory penalties create a sort of fear that restrains men who are not naturally disposed to vice, from committing crime when tempted and temporarily contemplated; but to a mind so organized that there is a tendency to crime, or one so educated by environment as to think he has a right to plunder the rich and prosperous or coerce those who differ from him in opinion or belief, the penalty does not restrain by fear; but operates to make the party more cautious, and causes him to exert his faculties in the commission of other crimes, the better to circumvent the law and make his chance for success more certain. It is not fear for or regard to the punishment that affects him, but the desire to not fail and be defeated in his attempt to make gain or accomplish his purposes.

This disregard of and contempt for penalties, is a natural

result of fixed penalties for offences regardless of the individual or the facts, as well as the uncertainty of the punishment. If the penalty could be so provided as to be graded to the individual and the facts in each case, and the question of reform be left out of sight—except so far as the place, manner and surroundings attending the punishment might operate to influence the offender—the indifference and contempt with which the criminally inclined now view the fixed penalties as a means for moral reformation, would be much less than it is now.

When one violates the law who does not know the law, he cannot be readily made to understand that he is morally wrong ; but an ignorant violation in the effect on others and on the objects of the law, is the same as a wilful violation. Punishment follows violations of natural laws, whether violated purposely or ignorantly. The idiot who thrusts his hand into the fire is burned the same as he would be if he knew the fire would burn it and thrust it in purposely. So with the civil law; the evil to society follows and operates to the injury of the innocent, whether the law be violated through ignorance or design. In either case the public order is disturbed and repetition is to be prevented by punishment. The law allows no plea of ignorance. Its penalties are fixed and its standard arbitrary. But the standard may be changed next month, or next year, or it may remain in force and be a dead letter by reason of a change in the public opinion.

If we are to afford protection by the infliction of penalties on offenders, it would be cruelty to inflict pain on the ignorant violator of law, and it would be absurd to do so as punishment when there was no moral guilt ; and doubly absurd to do so with a view to reformation, there having been no intentional departure from obedience to offence, the offender not knowing his act was unlawful. In case of the wilful offender, the punishment must be to impress on the culprit a consciousness of the power of the law, the will of those who observe it, the absolute necessity for obedience if the offender desires to have liberty and the exercise of individual rights. If reformation comes, it comes from like motives to those that prompted the crime—personal gain ; because he thinks it will be a personal gain to obey instead of infringing the law ; whether better perceptions and more wisdom enable him to see it, or whether mere selfishness induces him to obey the law, aside from moral improvement. The wilful violator of law will reform under punishment if he is so constituted as to comprehend and believe that it will be best to obey the law thereafter and he desires the best. Unless he is so constituted and does desire the best, moral reformation cannot be reached by punishment. There may be some elements in him that can be found and through which a reformation can be effected, but unless they be found moral reformation will not follow punishment, however inflicted.

Take the boy begotten and reared in the slums of the city, of ignorant, vicious parentage, bred amid vice, grown to manhood without scholastic education, and his associations continually evil. He sees evidences of culture, business, and comfort, all around him ; but between him and the intelligent, refined and prosperous, there is an impassable gulf. His thoughts even cannot pass it, for he has no personal knowledge of the other side. As to all that, it is in a foreign land where he knows neither the language nor the customs. Of constitutions, legislatures, laws, courts, trades, commerce, finance, the arts, morality, dignity, honor, he knows little or nothing. To him, a court and a prison are things to be avoided because they deprive him of the power to exercise his will. To him, the wise and prosperous are made so by plundering others, and it is just to rob them in any way he can. Right and wrong to him have a signification entirely at variance with the commonly received construction. Tell him how a law is made and what for, and read it to him, and his understanding of it would be nothing like that intended to be conveyed to him. He would be like the Indian who was being taught to read in the New Testament in his own language and translate into English, and was given the parable of the prodigal son and it was explained to him in its allegorical sense. This was his translation : "Old man—heap money—two boys. One boy no wait. Take heap money—go away. Have big drunk—money all gone—go home. Old man glad—make music—eat heap." That was all. Not the slightest perception of the lesson sought to be con-

veyed by the parable, nor was his mind capable of comprehending it, however presented. Take this boy I have described
and put him on trial for crime. He has violated the statute
and must be punished. But the punishment will not educate
him nor restrain morally, nor reform him. It will only make
him more wary and dangerous.

Take another from the same element, of different make-up.
He has quick perceptions, firmness, caution, secretiveness, and
is ambitious to be rich, but has no moral or reverential elements. He acquires some school education and begins to
look out for property. He may become an accomplished burglar, or forger, or may head some business and become an accomplished villain under broadcloth and fine linen. He knows
the law and violates it knowingly; trusting partly to chance,
partly to his own ability to escape; but driven on by his peculiar mental composition to the end he finally reaches. He is
dangerous to the public order and must be punished. He fears
punishment only as an interruption; a closing of the door to
further gain. If any moral considerations are active, it is because they affect his pride and his lessened chances of return
to his position where he can accumulate. No feelings of honor
are wounded. No sense of degradation because he has done
that which was wrong in itself, however considered, in a worldly
sense or in a religious light. Statutory punishment to him
will not reform him. The material to build on never existed
and cannot be created by punishment. At the end of the punishment he will go into a grade lower, where his abilities will
be used to obtain a position as a leader in a grosser grade of
offences, and he will become all the more dangerous.

Take another class—the brutal. The animals, on which
brute force alone makes impression. The class that will drown
in the pump room, and will yield only to the whip or the rack.
Crime is the natural and only outlet for such energy as they
possess. Reform is impossible. They have no lot or part in
life but to prey on mankind and disregard all law. Of right
and wrong they have no practical perception. They must be
restrained, but statutory punishment is lost on them. Physical
punishment operates not to reform, and only so far as fear of
torture shall keep them in order while in prison.

Take another—the semi-intelligent and weak-minded. The half-made intellect, and yet no fool, with certain shrewdness and quick perception in some directions; ability to reason well on some things to a limited extent. With firmness and a few other elements he would be good and useful, though not bright; but as he is, can be easily led and has no real perception of vice or the true relation of right and wrong as commonly understood. He is found and used by criminals. He follows and obeys them and does as directed, exercising his faculties under command. Should fortune cast him among the wise and honorable, he drops into his rut of subordination and exercises his faculties there under command. Detect him in crime and statutory punishment would not reform him; once free, he would fall under influences chance might throw around him and become the willing tool of those who could mislead.

Last, take those born and reared under favorable circumstances, but so organized as to possess criminal tendencies, or that lead to recklessness as to right and wrong, and that education has failed to eradicate. They will be likely to drift into the channels of offence and become amenable to the law. But restraint and punishment, as now most largely practised under statutory penalties, with their association have no reliable elements that lead to reform.

From these classes come most of the criminals. And in all instances they are the victims of a state of relations and facts for which they are not responsible. They are the results of causes, over which causes they had little or no control. Had these different persons been taken when young and been developed under favorable training and surroundings, while congenital evils might not have been eradicated, they would have been, probably, placed in a position where they would have been comparatively harmless. But having been developed as they are, reform is out of the question by any statutory penalties inflicted as punishment. As I have sought to show in previous chapters, the origin of the evil to be dealt with lies in the unlimited and unrestrained sexual license sanctioned by legal marriage, and mere animal propagation. Trying to reform the issue by statutory penalties is like trying to make a leaky steam engine work reliably when supplied from a boiler filled with dirty, greasy water.

The secret of prohibition of crime lies first, in an education, producing mental balance, and the proper location of persons when so educated as well as during education ; and second, in perpetual restraint where education fails to establish a mental balance.

A formidable difficulty to be contended with lies in the fact that, with the evil-minded and ignorant, liberty is used as if it were unlimited license—construing liberty to mean license. Liberty to do right according to the established standard can in no case be construed to do other than right. I have discussed education for restoration or creation of a mental balance in the chapters referring to Mentality and Mental Pathology, and the principles there laid down are applicable to convicts, with chances for reform proportioned to the impressibility of the individual and the firmness to practice the lessons learned. So far as natural defects can be thus supplied, so far will prohibition be accomplished. If they cannot be supplied, there is no success, the individual at large will prey upon his fellows, and prohibition will lie only in perpetual restraint.

If, in the exercise of individual liberty allowed, the privilege is abused, it cannot be left to be construed and treated as license, and should be at once cut off by personal imprisonment. Not as punishment, but as a necessity in the preservation of orderly government. The theologian can take no exception, for that is his theory of punishment. "Having been given the gift of life and having abused it, you shall be cut off forever," is his doctrine. The moralist can take no exceptions, because morality cannot live where evil has license, and safety lies only in perpetual separation. The ideas of charity, sympathy, sentiment, have no connection with the subject matter. They may come in and be considered in the prison, and there also the idea of punishment may be entertained as a means for preserving discipline; but none of them can rightfully or naturally enter into any consideration for the primary disposition of the public offender, nor for the final disposition of him if education fails to restore a mental balance, making him tend to right in impulse and action. (I mean such education as can be directed to that end.)

We find in all relations of life, that when favors are extended on conditions, with forfeiture in case of breach of conditions, the tendency of efforts is to retain or secure the favors by observing the conditions. Where forfeiture occurs it is held up by others having knowledge of it as a warning and example; but it is not to be considered as punishment, and if so considered would lose its tendency to maintain a disposition to observe conditions. Apply it to a class in school, striving for honors. Suppose that the failure to obtain them were to be regarded as punishment; what would be the moral effect of offering honors for the best deportment, diligence, and perfection in lessons? Half an eye can see that it would be demoralizing to the last degree. But offered on condition that they must be earned by good conduct, and the entire stimulus is toward moral ends guided by moral ambition.

Organized society gives each indvidual the gift of liberty, consistent with the equal rights of others and the public order. When the gift is abused society should take it back and prohibit its use in hands that abuse it; not as punishment, but as a forfeiture by breach of the conditions on which the favor is extended. The statutory system, or plan, or theory, of punishment for offences now in force, restores the favors after a fixed, temporary forfeiture, whether the offender be any more trustworthy or not; and this temporary forfeiture is miscalled punishment, and leaves the offender in the position to *compel the state to restore the favor*, though he may announce that he will again misuse and abuse it. As punishment it is a fallacy, and as an element in reformation it is an absurdity.

Under the statutory system of penalties there is no certainty of infliction on offenders. There is no equality in inflictions. There is exultation in those who escape, or who escape lightly, and a constant sense of injustice and a desire for revenge, in those who are condemned, or who suffer severe penalty where others in like cases have escaped, or escaped with light sentence. In both there is contempt for the law and constant efforts to evade and defeat it by any means. But if it could come to be understood, that breach of the conditions on which liberty is enjoyed, will forfeit the privilege absolutely, as a result, with no right whatever to restoration, and no hope only at the will of the state, we might reasonably look for more caution, more fear of forfeiture, and less cases of offence. The absence from the public of those put away and their non-return, with the knowledge of that fact by those remaining at large, would exert a powerful influence in the prohibition of crime. Remove from the statute all idea of punishment as a result of offence, and let it be understood that the right to live in the world with their fellow men, would be forfeited in case of offence, and that thenceforth they would be exiles to prison walls, prison discipline and prison labor, and men who could reflect at all would pause before taking the chances of incurring the forfeiture.

Punishment, as I have intimated, is something pertaining to prison discipline and belongs inside the prison walls. As contemplated by the statutes with its system of penalties—and published for the information of all—it is much like telling a sick man who is regarded as dangerously ill, that you are going to make him more dangerously sick, with the expectation of curing him. That would tend to a fatal end rather than a favorable one; or, it is like breaking still worse a broken vessel as a means of restoring it. Properly understood, punishment is something that swiftly and certainly follows wrongdoing, bringing personal danger and physical suffering of a character to create a dread of having it repeated, A threat of it creates no dread unless two things concur in connection with it—the certain power to inflict it and the certainty that it will be inflicted. This can be done in prison in aid of discipline. But it cannot concur in connection with the statute, for the state has not the certain power to arrest the offender or the certainty of inflicting the penalty when an arrest is made. Therefore, as I have asserted, punishment by the state by means of specific penalties should be entirely done away with, except so far as forfeiture of the right to liberty, and commitment to prison without any definite limit, may operate as punishment, on such as may be reformed and eventually be again trusted with liberty.

In the prison there can and should be punishment for breach

of discipline. It may be by forfeiture of favors or privileges, or of personal comforts; by added burdens; and with the brutal and devilish who have no moral elements to which appeal can be made, by inflicting physical pain. There, certainty of power to inflict and certainty of infliction can concur with the promise of it, in case of offence for which penalty is proper. There, too, it can be apportioned and graded to the individual and the facts in each case, with a certainty of justice as nearly as human judgment can perceive. There, charity, pity, sympathy, benevolence, and sentiment, governed by common sense, can be so manifested as to mingle with discipline, act as solvents, mediums for understanding, stimulants to higher thoughts and better impulses, invigorants, to aid good resolves, and material aids in the hands of wise and humane officials, toward reformations in those where reform is possible. In such a place and under such relations and conditions only can a true idea of punishment obtain, and a practical use be made of it, either for discipline alone, or for discipline as an aid to reformation.

Under the head of Prisons and Reformation I may further consider the subject of punishment to some extent in those connections, but in this review I desire to emphasize the argument that the present statutory enactments that provide determinate penalties with a view to punishment, not only fail of the object, but are inimical to every correct idea and purpose of punishment. If reformation is the object—as it should be —it tends to prevent it. If the convict is not reformable, it allows him to demand a restoration to liberty at the end of the term, regardless of his fitness for it. It places the state, the criminals, and society, all in a false position and maintains false relations, to the detriment of all three. Therefore, all fixed penalties should be abrogated. Provisions should be made for the proper confining of offenders, by such prisons as are needed, and on conviction the offender should be committed as an enemy to liberty. The temporary and final dispositions to be made of him should be determined by facts, the first as developed at the time of conviction, and the last as they may be developed after commitment.

CHAPTER XIII.

THE subject of prisons, in the thoughts of the legislative mind, has been on the same plane with the ideas of punishment by the state, by means of fixed penalties; "confined at hard labor for the period of —— years," etc. There, to have the head and face shaved, a zebra suit of coarse clothes, a narrow cell with hard bed, silence, coarse food and mere animal existence with hard labor. It was for all alike, for long time, male and female, old and young, the least offensive and through every grade down to the vilest, differing only in the term. Later years have made separations. Some states have separate institutions for the sexes and for the young offenders; but in many the old forms prevail. A few have reformatories and some classifications; but in all the sentence is still limited and fixed, though subject to earlier determination, dependent on the prisoner himself. In some additions have been made to personal comfort and convenience, improvement in the food furnished, in hospital arrangements, disposition of sewage and waste, water supply, and enlargement of liberty by release from restraints, with means for amusement, acquisition of knowledge, and other things to make life less brutal and more endurable. But the general idea of punishment by the state prevails entirely, and the idea of reformation has obtained only a partial footing, and that mostly in the conduct of prisons by the wardens and managers, who are doing their best in the direction of reformations that they can, under the legal provisions as they exist and by which they are bound. But profitable progress cannot be made, of a permanent character, until the legislature can be made to understand that prisons must be constructed and adapted to the processes needed for reformation, as well as for safe keeping of prisoners; and that requires the recognition of some facts to which the legislative will is opposed whenever those facts present themselves. The first one is the fact of cost. As a practical fact legislation goes too much on the ground that public parsimony is public economy; and often it pinches hardest where liberality is true economy, and is most liberal when pinching would be economy. It will appropriate twelve hundred dollars a room (in some cases four thousand dollars) to build a hospital for a thousand insane people, and money without limit to provide for and treat the patients, where no systematic labor is or can be done by the inmates; but it will pinch to the last possible limit of force, in providing for one thousand convicts who are all to labor, and be treated for an insanity more dangerous, needing greater care and skill, and the provisions required are of far more consequence to the public welfare, than in case of the insane. A moral obliquity exists in this case as well as in another case I have spoken of. It is of far more consequence that the public offenders should be cured than that the insane and demented should be, or that they should be safely kept. The crime classes occupy a relation to the state more vital than the latter do or can. The provisions made for the insane are, in some respects, uselessly extravagant. Those for the offenders are, in some respects, senselessly penurious. The question of costs for proper prison arrangements, should be a secondary consideration to the necessities in carrying out the constitutional mandate to found the criminal code "on the principle of reformation." The existing prisons are, in many ways, unfitted for that purpose, and some of them wholly so.

The prison population is increasing faster in proportion than the general population. The characteristics of the criminals and of the criminal classes are changing from the old types. The regulations as to labor are everywhere changing more than anything else. The theories of prison authorities as to the different systems for prisons—the congregate, the solitary, and the wholly reformatory plans—as well as the theories regarding labor in prisons, are in an antagonistic condition that is not favorable to discovery of the best, at an early time in the future. There is a conflict between old experience under old methods and young experience under new methods among prison officials, as well as between old sentiment and enthusiasm and new sentiment and enthusiasm, between theologians and humanitarians in the religious world of reformers. Amid the confusion it is not easy to get a foundation steady and still enough, to obtain a good observation of any new suggestions, so they can be fairly examined by themselves. It is of importance that it be done, however.

The demagogism of machine, partisan politics that encouraged and dragged elements of the labor problem into the prison, and to secure the votes of laboring men finally established a foolish sentiment to the effect that prison labor competed with outside labor, to the injury of the latter; to some extent secured abolition of labor in the prisons, and created a baseless opinion resulting in some legislation of a character dangerous to the peace and well-being of society, in an effort to force labor from the prisons. If those in the prisons were at labor outside the competition would be greater, and to support convicts without labor is a greater detriment to outside labor, than all the labor that can be done in prisons would be.

The purpose of imprisonment must be borne in mind. It is to protect society and government from the disorderly elements; to reform those elements and make them orderly where possible; and to keep them in prison if not reformable. With this before us, we must see what those disorderly elements are just as they must be dealt with, in order to know what kind of prison is needed. Convicts may be classed under five heads:

1. Those who are innocent and wrongly convicted, with those who are accidental offenders; who have been ignorant of the law or have misunderstood it, and have had no intention to commit a crime; although they might have known their act was not in strict accordance with a high sense of honor. A case like this for instance. A, has a business and property and is embarrassed. With a little time he can extricate himself; but without more time than his creditors will give when they learn his condition he must become bankrupt. He gets some friend to act as dummy for him, and for a pretended or inadequate consideration sells out to him, to hold until he can turn himself. The friend does not know that it is crime to be

a party to such a transaction, and neither party have any intention or idea of defrauding any creditor, but intend to pay all in full; while in law it is an offence to hinder creditors without intent to defraud. Had he known it, he would not have been a party to it. They are detected and convicted. There is no element of the criminal here, though the door is opened that leads to crime. But it obstructs the law in the general preservation of order, and is, therefore, unlawful. Or, take a case of assault and defence, where, in the excitement and heat of passion, the defence goes too far and mortally injures the assailant without any real intention to do so, and without any real necessity. He becomes the aggressor and is convicted of manslaughter. There was no criminal design or intention, only want of thought.

2. The criminals whose moral perceptions are such as will enable them to see that it is best to do right, and have moral will power enough to hold them in the channels of right when pointed out and they have been taught *how to make a living* while following those channels. This class is reformable.

3. Those with moral perceptions to recognize the wrong, and be willing to avoid it, but who cannot be taught to make a living while doing right. These will fall into crime again, or remain on the plane of pauperism, and propagate more like themselves.

4. Those who can comprehend right and wrong, who can make a living while acting right, but lack will-power, either to control their criminal impulses, or to resist temptation, or the persuasion of others of evil intentions. These cannot be trusted.

5. The brutal and vicious; and those with weak moral perceptions or none at all, whether they be intelligent or ignorant. Those with no moral anchorage to hold them and no elements or susceptibilities to which an appeal can be made, except that of fear of personal torture. With such, reformation is impossible.

In the first four classes will be found every grade of intelligence and kind of temperament that exists among the non-criminal class. They will come to the prisons, from the ignorant clod-hopper and the denizen of the city slums, to the educated country gentleman and the city-bred collegian; the pov-

erty-stricken youth with no chances for advancement, to the
rich man's child who has had every advantage, and been placed
in a position he could not fill, merely to gratify parental pride
and ambition; from the dunce to the genius; from the hap-
py-go-lucky, devil-may-care roysterer to the sullen and discon-
tented gambler; from the born human hog, to the delicate,
sensitive, refined organism that is instinctively gentlemanly :
yet all are unbalanced, and all drift into prison moorings because of an unbalanced mentality or unfortunate environment,
or of both.

It should not require any special wisdom to see that no one
kind of a prison can be proper to receive and treat all these :
or that no practical reformation can be effected in one prison
alone. And it follows as a necessity that a system of prisons
is required to carry out the commands of the fundamental law.
Those for juveniles and females, separate from those for men :
and enough as to all for necessary classification. This is
thoroughly carried out for the insane, and I repeat, and desire
to emphasize it, that it is of far more importance to the state
and the public that it should be done for the offending classes :
for, as factors in society and government, they bear far more
important relations to the state and the public welfare than
the insane do, and their cure or safe custody is of more importance in every way. A practical design for such a system
of prisons and for their proper management will be one solution of the " prison question " so far as convicts are concerned,
while such practical legislation as will prohibit or limit the
procreation of criminals and the elements that cause them,
will complete the solution of that question to the extent that
human effort can reach. Toward the subject of restriction
and prevention I have already offered suggestions. If, as the
generations have passed, legislation and education have brought
the changes from polytheism to monotheism, and from polygamy to monogamy, it would seem difficult to find reasons
why it cannot and should not effect a change from promiscuous
generation to stirpiculture. And if, in the progress already
made, legal extremes are resorted to, as we see in Utah to-day to
suppress a trifling matter of a few sporadic cases of plural marriages, practiced as part of a religious belief, far more wisely

and justly may we go to more extreme legal means, to suppress the appalling and epidemic evil of the production of millions of paupers, idiots and criminals. Not forgetting this imperative necessity, I wish to offer some further suggestions on the subject of prisons.

The first matter of importance is, the selection of a location. It should be such that perfect drainage, abundant water supply, and ready disposition of waste and sewage can be secured, and also be convenient to principal lines of transportation. It should be outside of the lines of any city or town; should have abundance of room—not less than one hundred or one hundred and fifty acres; should be a state reservation, exempt from any and all interference by any other organization or agency.

The reservation should be for state purposes alone; with no right of municipal or private corporations within it for any purpose whatever, except so far as the state may authorize. and use officials as agencies with corporate powers in government. At present some towns and cities have extended their limits and jurisdiction beyond and around penitentiaries, exercising absolute control on every side, and they can be approached only within and subject to the municipality and subject to its regulations. Such a situation and the relations incident are absurd to the extent of ridicule.

The prison should be built with a view to making escape impossible. To the preservation of health. To the purposes of varied industrial pursuits. To the education and moral elevation and development of the inmates, their classification into groups, and so that congregate or isolated conditions can be maintained to a necessary extent. There should be plenty of light; provisions for heating under complete regulating adjustments, sufficient for the lowest temperature, and also for ventilation. Sleeping cells should be located so plenty of sunlight can enter the court, and be excluded at will. Abundant provisions for extinguishment of fire, and for maintaining perfect cleanliness.

A prison involves all the elements and forces in operation in the outside world, and needs all that is there required, with the added elements the world would need if its inhabitants could escape from it and it was necessary to prevent them. The inmates are to be governed; and that involves laws, officials, armed forces, revenue, and productive industries. They must be housed, clothed, fed, instructed, doctored, and kept clean. That involves provisions for labor and means to earn money; hotel management; supplies for everything; conveyances, streets, vehicles, municipal management and supervision; besides schools, instructors, and everything to manage a world by itself, filled with a majority of disorderly inhabitants who are unwilling residents, who must live together there. To make such provisions calls for the highest skill in science and art, and for the best executive ability in arrangements and construction, and the best administrative ability in supervision and conduct. Permanency, utility, adaptability to the uses desired, future enlargement and additions, each and all are to be considered; *for this world will not cease to exist and will grow larger.*

I have said, the principal prison should be a receiving prison and reformatory, to which all first offenders should be sent, there to remain for experiment and trial. If it is decided that they are reformable, to be retained there until released on parole or pardon, or prove to be unreformable. The course of discipline must continue a matter of experiment for some time yet. It is being conducted here and abroad under different theories, and time, with local conditions, will modify methods, and ultimately develop the highest possibilities.

There should be a second and subordinate prison built on the same general plan, with a view to the perpetual confinement of the unreformable of the better classes; including the third and fourth classes I have designated. To this, all these unreformable convicts and all second offenders should be sent and kept. Some of them may, ultimately, develop evidences of possible reformation, and may be again removed to the reformatory and given further trial. So, second offenders may be found of this kind who may be again tried. Constant care and watchfulness on the part of the prison managers will be able to detect every case with reasonable certainty, and enable them to see that reformable characters have every opportunity.

In neither of these prisons should there be any marks or

badges of disgrace or humiliation. Proper uniform cannot be
so regarded. The interests of the convict and the government are identical, and the aim of government should be to
make the convict comprehend the true relations and objects.
They are not different from those existing in the insane, the
deaf and dumb, the blind and the feeble-minded asylums; or,
in fact, in the free schools. Each inmate has different mental
elements to be worked on and impressed to the same end and
for the same results. In each, it is to build up such mental
force as will enable the subject to go out into the world, secure
a living, and fill the place of an orderly citizen. In the criminal, a vicious element in the mentality is to be removed, moral
perception be created, with mental force to make the impulses
from them the dominant motive of action. Punishments—including corporal ones—can be restored to, to maintain discipline; but the idea of punishment by imprisonment and
labor for the state, should be wholly excluded. That idea of
punishment should exist only in the relations between the
convict and the governor of the prison, and must be left largely
to the governor's discretion under control of the prison board.
It should be inflicted only on his personal order, and under
his eye. Firmness, unvarying kindness, and no exhibitions of
temper, should at all times characterize the governor and
keepers. Whether the punishment be moral, mental or physical, a complete and full explanation of the relations, the rules
violated, the offence and to what it leads, and the object of
the punishment—to show that the new relations created by
the offence make punishment a necessity and a duty, and it
all results from the act of the offender himself—should be
made and strongly impressed on the offender; and his own
statement should be fully heard and the punishment be graded
to the offence and the peculiar character of the individual.
No subordinate or employé should be permitted to condemn
to punishment without personal order from the governor, nor
be ordered by the governor without the fullest interview and
explanation with and to the offender.

The convict is the ward and the apprentice of the state. To
reiterate somewhat, he lacks a mental balance, disturbs the
public order, and the state shuts him up. It offers him protec-

tion in person, estate and domestic relations, in return for his
honest performance of the duties of a citizen. Because of
natural tendency to vice (an infirmity, as much as that of an
insane ward), or weakness of will in resisting vicious influences,
(like the blind ward who cannot see his way), or of gross ignorance and inability to comprehend (like the deaf mute who
cannot hear to learn), he disregards his obligations and the
state puts him in prison out of harm's way. The interests of
both are identical; and that is, his reformation or enlightenment, release, and return to a citizen's place and duties. He
should be made to understand this relation and identity of interest between the state and himself, as clearly as is possible.
That the state has no object or desire to inflict pain on him,
or to disgrace or humiliate him. That he is bad, and the state
shuts him away from society and gives him a chance to become
good; and that he cannot fight the state and win. Or, he has
been weak or unwise. If he will became strong and learn to
be wise, he can go back to liberty. If not, he can never go
back, but must stay and work for the state, and help take care
of himself and his class. The state is his best, his truest, his
most liberal and strongest friend. To keep it so when outside,
he must be orderly. If he does not, it is still his friend; for it
puts him away, protects him against injury to himself and
others, makes him useful and gives him shelter, food and raiment. Such an impression—if made—must and will remove
every other inimical to it; and a comprehension and realiza-
tion of this relation and object in the mind of the convict, will
effect reform if reform be possible. If it does not, nothing
else will. In aid of it, while under restraint, the convict must
be made useful and industrious; be furnished employment
adapted to his physical condition and mental capacity; be
classed with those least likely to discourage, or exercise an unfavorable influence over him. While the kinds of employment
must be limited, they should be considered as a means in reformation, and opportunity be given for change and modifications
as may be found for the best, from time to time.

The convict should be made to understand that the prison
is still the state, lessened in dimensions, but the same relations
exist between him and the prison authorities representing the

law, and his labor and general conduct as if he existed outside, and order and duty in the prison are as necessary to favors and protection there as it was necessary outside. That disorder will put him in still closer bounds; cut off still more of liberty and personal favors, and bring on him still greater restraints and burdens; while order and good conduct will enlarge boundaries and privileges, until reform will open the doors and restore him to the larger privileges of the state.

Suitable managers, foremen, instructors, and assistants should be furnished, as is done in any other department or asylum; or in an armory, navy yard, military or naval school, postal department, or any other place where citizens are to be made fit for the uses of government, whether as citizens or employés. And if it is necessary in the charge of those who are sane and at liberty and orderly, in any business of government, it is all the more necessary in case of the unsound and disorderly in government prisons. It is not possible to be right in saying that, a bad and disorderly person is to be turned adrift because he is so, nor to be right in saying that, where government takes him into custody because he is so, it shall treat him as other than as an apprentice, working under compulsion, until he demonstrates his ability to work for himself. Government is compelled to take him into custody, as it does one violently or murderously insane; and being in custody, his bad tendencies do not change these relations at all, only to the extent required to make proper provisions for his care and cure, or care and usefulness, or at least harmlessness, if incurable.

There should be a third prison for the worst class, and they should be there separately confined for life, but under similar rules as in the other prisons, but adapted to them. They should have favors and comforts proportioned to conduct. Even there, development of latent forces may, in time, entitle the convict to a trial in the second prison, and even in the first. In the third prison, vice and devilishness being the prime factor in the make-up of the inmates, the supplies should be of a character to give common comforts and no more. Food should be nutritious and abundant, and efforts by the convict to rise above his normal level in conduct should be rewarded by extended favors; but as reform is hopeless the convict should be regarded as a burden to the state, and entitled to no consideration only common animal comforts, in return for the labor he should be required to perform. This class of convicts are like a dangerous fulminate, or a defective gun or steam boiler. There is no telling when or on what occasion they may explode; and the provisions for and care of them require to be of the highest order of safety, and the latitude of privileges allowed must be limited and well guarded.

In each prison ample provision should be made for labor suited to the purpose of the prison. In the middle and incorrigible prisons, labor should be used as in any other business enterprise, for the best interest of the state. To employ and benefit the inmates and pay expenses of the penal department as far as possible; and it should be conducted on any plan that will best serve that end; or on different, or on several plans. In the first prison, labor should be used in business carried on for the state alone. And this may be done on any plan or several plans. The state may let a contract to some party or firm to conduct any branch of business; but the employés should be wholly under state control and direction. There should be no hiring of convicts to contractors in this prison, but contracts to manufacture so much, using convicts as employés, and the labor estimated at its value as part of the investment, which the state furnishes and for which the manufacturer pays, taking the product. Or contracts to furnish so much material, the foremen and teachers; work and teach the convicts and pay so much per piece, or other quantity, for the product. The state should control the plant for all labor carried on. Others might work by the piece. Others still, on state account, entirely. Some convicts having families might be allowed wages, taxed for expenses, and the residue earned net be given to the families. This prison should be conducted with a view to reformation entirely; and while economy should be observed closely there should be no effort to make profit for the state at the expense of the main object. As in the case of the blind, the object is, to make sound citizens out of defective ones with ability to gain a living. In making this repeated comparison to impress the idea of a

principle, I do not wish to be understood as classifying the
blind on a moral level with the convict. The former should
be much better provided for than the latter. The fact of the
vice in the convict should not be lost sight of, nor his lesser
claim to charity. The purely unfortunate like the blind and
deaf mutes, are entitled to the best that charity can give.
But the convict is also an unfortunate in most instances; and
until he proves to be unreformable, he, too, needs charitable
considerations, as well as those that belong to the policy of
state aid, looking to his cure, but of a less liberal character.
Beyond that, mere personal comfort answers the demand, and
with the worst class a plain degree of that.

There can be no question but that, strong bodily vigor and
health are necessary to a clear moral perception; and it also
cannot be questioned that a majority of convicts do not possess that vigor and health among those who have been reared
amid the comforts of life. That, a restoration to health, or the
production of it where it has not existed, helps to produce a
moral tendency, and in the theory and experience of the best
scientific ability the special cultivation of strong bodily vigor
is one of the greatest auxiliaries in reforming convicts. In
this view the receiving prison should possess every facility for
the production of vigorous health. The same idea should be
kept in view in respect to labor as a means in advancing the
convict. He should be taught to understand the value and
uses of labor; not only as a means of livelihood, but as a factor
in education and intellectual elevation. To take a pride in the
quality of his work; in adding to the market value by his care
and skill; and the improvement in himself that surely will
come from the energies created by such a use of his faculties
and hands.

The three prisons should be entirely separate, though they
may be all be located on the same farm, or in close proximity.
As to the arrangement of buildings, I have not seen any that
seemed to me to be such as would best serve the purpose.
Either the buildings should enclose an open square and all
face it, with no obstructions in the center, or a large square
should be inclosed, with buildings separately located in the
central part in parallel lines for the congregate prison, with

liberal roadways between and enclosed covered crossways above from one to the other, and a broad area on the outside unobstructed to view or use ; and no building should approach or connect with the outer wall anywhere, except the offices at the main entrance. (For the isolated prison—if used—perhaps the radiate plan from a common center, is best.) There should be a liberal parade ground, and military drill should constitute a part of the discipline. There should be room to devote to landscape effects and adornments, admission to which should be among the favors. I am not pretending to present designs for a prison, but suggestions in mere outline in connection with the intention expressed by the law, that "the principle of reformation" shall be the basis for legislation on the subject of crime and the disposition of criminals ; and in a work like this, even those must be very limited. If what I have said in the preceding chapters is considered, showing as it does the elements to be dealt with in seeking to change the mentality and mentalisms of a human being, nearly or entirely matured, in each case there will be the origin and growth of existing conditions ; with the attendant facts of the environment up to that time ; domestic, social, industrial, educational, moral and religious, which, united, have produced the conditions. The new environment furnished by the state is the final condition which all that has preceded has added to those attending the convict to that time. An effort is to be made, using this new environment to examine, analyze, and endeavor to so manipulate the subject as to create a different mentality and consequently new mentalisms. Such a perception of political, social and individual relations, duties and obligations, as will enable the individual to practically adapt himself to them, with the impulses to do so, and continue to maintain them. The prison and its provisions is the means by which this result is to be accomplished, and it is easy to see that, the requirements are such as to demand the very highest order of human skill in designing the details and carrying them out. That, to secure the greatest possible success neither expense or time should be considered. The state is powerful enough, its resources are ample enough, its orderly existence is at stake, and it needs only to cut loose from fallacious precedent, recognize facts as they really are, and deal with them practically. Whatever can aid in accomplishing the best results desired should be provided, looking steadily at the conditions as they are, and as they will be, and as they are sought to be made. The productions and creations of the past now existing, should be disregarded and cast aside whenever they fail to harmonize and entirely unite with the present aims and purposes.

There is no *mean* in the "prison question," even when confined to prisons themselves. The whole subject is a mass of extremes. With the criminal at large there is anarchy; therefore, he must be confined. In confinement new extremes arise, and to meet them the law has fixed confinement as a *punishment*, with a paradox that it shall be on the principle of reformation, and after a fixed period the confinement shall cease, regardless of reformation. As a new extreme we must abrogate the law and repudiate the idea of confinement as punishment and regard simply the idea of safety in it. Then the true object of the law—confinement for safety and the purpose of reformation and until there is reformation—is to be carried out and the prison is the means to be provided for that end and purpose, and no other means can be provided. Therefore, legislation providing for the prison takes the first position in the order of precedence in reform, and demands the highest consideration government can give in its provisions for maintaining the purposes of government. Having defined what acts shall be regarded as crime, having provided for examination of those who are arrested as offenders so as to secure justice, and commited them to prison, having provided for a system of identification of those who have been so committed, and having provided the prison, the legislative power is exhausted in this portion of the provisions for government. Everything done and that can be done centralizes and crystallizes for good and useful ends or for bad and vicious ones *in the prison*. The two ends desired being safety and reformation, the wisdom of the provisions for the prison throughout, will be demonstrated in the results; hence, the prison ranks all other considerations.

CHAPTER XIV.

REFORMATION.

THE effort to reform criminals may be compared to the conversion of iron into steel; with the difference that some kind of steel can be made out of nearly every kind of iron, but every kind of criminal cannot be reformed. In the conditions, process and requirements, there is a strong analogy. In making steel the first thing is, to have the knowledge necessary to commence and continue the process, with the right kind of furnace and other means. The next is, the time. The master workman then examines his iron. If he has to take a mixed and uncertain lot, he must examine, decide upon its quality and characteristics, decide on what it will make and how to treat it, and provide for testing the results of the process from time to time. Different lots and kinds of iron will require difference in the process of treatment, although all on one general principle. To force in and combine the carbon with the iron, until its nature is changed to the new substance called steel, is the object. If it is the first conversion into blister steel, it must be put through a further process under the trip-hammer to make it homogeneous in quality; restore it after the disintegrations caused by the process of the furnace. If it is the second conversion of making cast steel by breaking up and melting, other provisions must be made. And so when made, in preparing the steel for use; processes for tempering and testing must be resorted to with great care; and until found to be properly made and tempered, it is not to be put upon the market for use.

Almost exactly the same procedure and requirements are necessary in efforts to reform the criminal; whether it be a first reformation or that of a backslider. As a change of the natural character and order of particles takes place in the case of the iron and steel, so a change takes place in the character and

order of the tissue in the criminal. As it must be examined
and understood before and during the process to know what
to do and what is the result of progress from time to time, so
with the culprit; it must be ascertained what kind of defects
exist, what is sound, what is not sound, and the effects of
treatment be watched and known. If there is conversion to
reform it must be perfected by trial and consolidation, to see
if it is true and permanent conversion. If not, the convict is
not to be turned loose upon the public as fit to be trusted as a
citizen and orderly member of society.

To effect reform requires practical knowledge in many directions, sound common sense, firmness, kindness, and unweary-
ing patience. One must be able to read character; must know
men; must be acquainted with the principles involved in mental and social science; and should possess a good medical
education. The first important consideration is, the health
and bodily vigor of the subject. The next is, the extent
and character of his knowledge, perception and reasoning
powers. The next is, his antecedents, and lastly his idiosyncrasies of body and mind. This may be learned in a
short time or it may take much time. When learned, the
kind of subject to be dealt with is known and the process
to be followed can be decided on. Having got to his level
it now remains to be seen if he can be made to comprehend the reformer; and if the latter can force into him the
knowledge that will give him the necessary perceptions and
impulses to guide him on the way to reform, and change him
from bad to good, as the carbon is forced into the iron to convert it into steel. And if done, whether he can be so confirmed
in its use as to make it permanent, as the steel is consolidated
under the trip-hammer. Here will begin the study and practice of mental pathology as the main process in directing the
reformer. It may be necessary to change the character of
brain tissue, and it will be necessary to change the character
and operative force of brain ganglia, by developing the deficient, depressing the active force and the over active, and the
production of the harmony attendant on a balanced development of the higher faculties.

The vital forces of body and mind in a convict in prison,

especially at the time of entering, are in more or less depressed condition. The reformer begins with his patient under this disadvantage. The finer his organization the more sensitive and intelligent he is, the greater the depression; and more so in a first offender. With such persons the possibilities of release through reformation will be apt to create a hope that will tend to remove this depression. With other temperaments, and especially such as fail in good efforts and relapse more or less, it will be apt to increase. The position of the warden and moral instructor will be no sinecure if the work is done by them that is necessary to effect reform in those that are reformable. The entire revolution in the relations that would follow the abolition of the present methods, and the substitution of prisons and sentence on the principle of reformation, would necessitate an entirely different course of procedure from that now followed, in efforts to effect reforms. More or less individual work would be required in studying the individual; giving advice suited to his special condition; offering help and encouragement in each case suited to it; as well as the discipline and knowledge that would be for classes and for all.

Deception, voluntary and involuntary, would be a serious factor to deal with. The promises and beliefs of the sanguine and sincere might mislead themselves and their governors as well. So, those of the deceitful might. And here would come in the testing experiments; the tempering of the metal; the trials in various ways to determine if the reform is actual, with firmness and moral strength behind it to maintain it; or if it be real, but of the brittle kind that will not stand the strain to which it will be subjected; or if it be an appearance only—pretended but not real.

To emphasize somewhat the ideas I wish to convey, I will refer to a few facts as given in the annual report to the legislature of New York, by the board of managers and officers of the reformatory at Elmira, January, 1890, as to the inmates of that prison. The statistics include 3636 prisoners. None admitted who are over 30 years of age; convicts between 16 and 30. First, facts tending to affect the mental and physical organisms in generation; giving the vital origin of tissue and arrangement of the vital centers.

Of epileptic or insane ancestry, there was 13.7 per cent. Of drunkenness in ancestry, clearly traced, 38.7 per cent. Of doubtful drinking ancestry, 11.1 per cent. Of temperate ancestry, 50.2 per cent. Of ancestry with no education, 13.6 per cent. Of ancestry that could simply read and write, 38.1 per cent. Of ordinary common school education, or more, 43.8 per cent. Of high school education, or more, 4.5 per cent. Of pauperized ancestry there was 4.8 per cent. Of those with no accumulations, 77 per cent. Of those who were forehanded, 18.2 per cent. Of ancestry who were servants or clerks, 10.4 per cent. Of those who were common laborers, 32.6 per cent. Of those who were mechanical workers, 36.9 per cent. Of those who were engaged in traffic, 17.7 per cent. Of professionals, lawyers, doctors, preachers and teachers, 2.4 per cent.

It will be noted that there are more educated than ignorant, more mechanics and traders than laborers and servants, more with temperate than intemperate habits; while the main body was on the plane of poverty.

Next, as to environment at birth, and the after home life, when first impressions were made, and growth and development of brain ganglia fixed the mentality and mentalisms of the individual. Of those where the home character was positively bad, 51.8 per cent. Of those where it was fair only, there were 39.9 per cent. Of those where it was good, there were 8.3 per cent. Of 1534 convicts, who were homeless, there occupied furnished rooms in cities, 25.4 per cent. There lived as itinerants in cheap boarding places, 18.2 per cent. There lived with their employers, 21.6 per cent. There lived as rovers and tramps, 34.8 per cent. There left home before ten and up to about fourteen years, 42.2 per cent. There were at home until the time of crime, 57.8 per cent. As to associations there were, positively bad, 56.9 per cent. Not good, 39.6 per cent. Doubtful, 1.8 per cent. Good, 1.7 per cent.

As to education, the illiterates were, 19.5 per cent. Those who could read and write with difficulty, 49.9 per cent. Those with ordinary school education, 26.9 per cent. Those with high school education, or more, 3.7 per cent.

As to mental capacity, those with deficient natural capacity, were 2 per cent. Those with fair capacity only, were 21.7

per cent. Those with good capacity, were 63.2 per cent. Those with excellent capacity, were 13.1 per cent. As to culture, those who had none were 43.2 per cent. Those who had very slight, were 28.6 per cent. Those who had ordinary, were 25.2 per cent. Those who had much, were 3 per cent.

Then comes susceptibility to moral impressions and those who had positively none were 36.2 per cent. Those who had possibly some (which means practically none, in effect,) 36.1 per cent., making a total of 72.3 per cent. Of those ordinarily susceptible there were 23.4 per cent. Of those specially susceptible there were 4.3 per cent.

Lastly, and indicative of the absence of a mentality that theological or religious reasoning and teaching can impress, until a complete mental revolution in a physical arrangement can be effected, we have the lamentable fact that, of those with moral sense as shown under examination, either filial affection, sense of shame, or sense of personal loss—all the elements that will feel a moral effect of punishment by the present legal methods, and be improved by it—there were those who had absolutely none, 49.3 per cent. Those who had possibly some. (which means none for all practical purpose and effect,) 30.6 per cent. Being an appalling total of nearly 80 per cent Ordinarily sensitive, only 15.2 per cent. And especially sensitive, 4.9 per cent.

It is highly probable that this is a more favorable showing than can be made by most other prisons. The great substratum of petty offenders that fill the city prisons and houses of correction, and work-houses; that are sent up for short terms, and that furnish some of the criminals who finally reach the Reformatory, would make a much less favorable showing in intelligence and moral perception, if examined and classified with equal care, while they largely outnumber the felons, and yet are on the crime levels, and in the outcome more dangerous to the moral well-being of society. But the same general condition runs throughout the crime class, and investigation up to this time seems to prove beyond the power of successful contradiction, the truth of the general statements I have made in the preliminary chapters of this work. And to clearly show as well, that reformation is possible, only through the means

of a new birth ; the creation of a new mentality by modification of the old ; by physical creation of a different character
of brain tissue through bodily changes by means of change of
environment and food, and mental impressions ; by teaching
and completely revolutionizing the individual, physically and
mentally.   That this can be done with some only and not all,
and that no complete reform can be perfected in any who have
no moral sense at the beginning.   To attempt it at all with a
determinate sentence to prison is, comparatively, waste of effort.   To turn the unreformed loose upon society is nothing
less than crime in the state, and makes government *particeps
criminis* in all the evils that follow from acts of the released
convict.

The tables from which the foregoing extracts were taken,
give the physical condition of the convicts as being, low and
coarse, 25.2 per cent.; medium, 37.2 per cent.; good, 37.6 per
cent.   In what was called good health, 86.2 per cent.   As a
basis for the work of reform we would have about 62.4 per
cent. of animals like a mule and horse with human intelligence.
Some, the coarse fibre of the mule in health, some, with the
more delicate fibre of the horse with health ; with no susceptibility to moral impressions, with no moral sense as to love of
home, shame, or personal loss.   It strongly emphasizes the
statement that the world within the prison is much like the
world without, and demands the same action to secure moral
supremacy—that is, *breeding* it as well as cultivating.   In the
prison the breeding is limited to secondary efforts to revolu-
tionize the results of vicious breeding at the start, and the cultivation of such material as has resulted.   It has been claimed
that eighty per cent. have been reformed.   I think the New
York and Massachusetts Reformatories have both made that
claim.   If the words, "discharged as reformed," be substituted,
they may be accepted.   But if we are to use the word "reformed," I doubt if twenty per cent. are reformed, or ever will
be.   And I apply that as the maximum to the criminal and
insane classes throughout.

So far, in this presentation of theories as contemplated in
this book, we have our prison, our convicts, and our general
knowledge of the material we have to deal with in our efforts

for reformation. We have the subjects of Mentality, of Marriage and Home, of the operation of Natural Forces, of Theology and its field of labor and power of impressing this mentality, and we have Mental Pathology and social conditions. We have the results of legislation and of domestic, social and political environment, and we have before us an outgrowth in the shape of this criminal, shut out from the world, and we are to begin to make him over and produce a self-sustaining moral intelligence out of him in place of the destructive immoral intelligence that has come of all these factors as a legitimate outgrowth. If we can do this, it will be the final solution of the prison question; the first solution being the prison for the experiment, and the last the physical and mental revolution of the inmate. It looks like an effort to reverse the operation of natural forces and make nature deny herself. If it can be done at all it must be done within the limits of the following conditions.

The convict must be regarded as a patient under treatment for a constitutional ailment, which can be cured only by means of a constitutional revolution, and the substitution of new physical and mental conditions. The first effort must be to enlarge his understanding. Give him an idea of government, its objects, organization, and methods of action. Next, the origin, growth and powers of society, and its relations to government. Next, his own position in and relations to both. The privileges, uses, and obligations of citizenship. The operation of natural forces along the planes on which the citizen moves in his relations to government and society, as an integral factor in each and both. The meaning of law and force and the relation between the superior and the subordinate under their operation, both natural and municipal. Unless he can be made to see these, there will be no foundation whatever on which to build. Progress for creation of a new mentality will be hopeless. If he be of an emotional nature, a clergyman might work on him and produce a hope of some unseen good and a fear of some unseen evil; but with eighty per cent. having " no moral sense, even such as shown under examination, either filial affection, sense of shame, or sense of personal loss," —to use the language of the Elmira report—what would be the prospect of creating such a moral sense, with a knowledge and firmness behind it to maintain it as a governing force to regulate conduct? The words in that item of the report are among the most sorrowful and depressing I have ever heard or read in connection with the subject of penology; and the lamentable truth they carry to the consciousness of the reflecting mind when searching the opening to a means of reform, call for the highest order of courage to meet them and continue the search.

A man who has been raised with no home surroundings would be a difficult subject on which to impress true ideas of domestic relations and life. The tables quoted, give between forty and fifty per cent. as being homeless. About seventy per cent. so illiterate that no true knowledge of home life could come through reading. Only eight per cent. had any good home surroundings. Less than two per cent. had good associations. A person of intelligence and moral impulses finds it difficult to realize such a condition. It is safe to say they cannot realize it, any more than a child can realize the position of an adult and the condition of the adult mind. And yet, for the purpose of reform the teacher must be able to realize it, to find the level of the criminal, to see things as he sees them, to reason about them as he reasons, to reach the conclusions he reaches, and feel the impulses he feels. He can neither teach or reform him without doing so. He cannot teach him as he would a child. The molder and wood bender will shape clay and wood because it is impressible; but let it be changed to stone by the process of petrifaction, and neither can mold or shape it for the purposes of clay or wood. The young child is the clay, the youth is the wood, the criminal convict in prison who has no sense of home is the petrifaction. The latter may be elastic and to some extent may be chiseled and bent into shape by various processes; but it is not the shape it could have been made before it became petrified. I lay the soft, pliant, fragrant cedar in the limestone stream, and the water will disintegrate and remove particle by particle, the gums, resins and woody fibre, and crystallized forms of carbonate of lime will be left in the places, and to all appearances the cedar still lies there; but it is not wood. This is the child begotten and grown to manhood amid the conditions stated in the report quoted. The prison receives him as you would remove the cedar from the stream to your laboratory. Do you believe you can take that cedar stone and restore it to wood? That is what the reformer can do if he can take this hardened body and mind and reform it. That is re-form—remould it. You may so treat the crystallized cedar as to make it useful and serve a good purpose somewhere ; but you cannot restore it to wood nor make it do the offices of wood as you could have done before it was laid in the stream.

But we will suppose you succeed in making the convict comprehend the true relations that attach to him as a member of society and in government, as you may teach a boy to solve a problem in surveying. It will avail little to the boy as a surveyor without any knowledge of the transit and the level. He must now be made acquainted with these and how to use them. So with the convict. Having knowledge of his relations to society and government, he must be taught how to use them and adapt himself to them, and make a living while doing so, and not exceed the privileges accorded to him. In the very first requisites are an intellectual as well as moral perception of the principles of right and wrong, according to the established standards. By what kind of teaching will this be accomplished, with eighty per cent. of the pupils having no natural susceptibility to moral impressions, and no moral sense? The only answer is, by creating the mental force that will produce moral sense and susceptibility to moral impressions. That requires complete organic change and arrangement. The supply of material and its arrangement in such order of combination as brain ganglia, as will permit of impressions that will create the faculties. The hidden physical and mental processes by which it may or can be done, may not be seen or comprehended, but to effect reform it must be done, and we can only work by the best lights we have. What I wish to enforce is, the idea that the change must be effected. No matter that it conflicts with all established ideas. No matter that it is contrary to the belief of the theologian and the humanitarian. It is a simple matter of fact about which there can be no dispute. Such conditions must be established in the body and brain of the convict, that the natural forces.

acting on the proper planes, will supply the defective faculties by building up the ganglions in which alone they can be located, and place them in harmonious action with others required to produce the desired result.

I am requested to take as a musical pupil, one who has no natural perception as to time or tune, and make a musician of him. He memorizes the lessons, and learns the keyboard of any instrument with fixed tones; and he becomes a mechanical performer. But every sound must be fixed and he must perform with a metronome before him. He cannot detect error in the tones by his ear, or emphasize the time by his instinct. In a word, he is a mere mechanical performer. With any instrument where the tones are not fixed as they are on a flute or piano, such as a violin, where he must select the stops, he could not play, for he would never know when his instrument was in tune, or his stop produced the right tone. If placed out to play for a regiment to march, he could not keep time or march in time himself. In the ranks he could mechanically keep step, but at no time be trusted alone to play or move in time. Now what perception of time and tune can be built up that will "reform" him, and make a musician of him that can be trusted? Wherein does he differ from the convict with no moral sense—no susceptibility to moral impressions? Can you go any farther in making the convict susceptible to moral impressions and moral force than you can in making the other susceptible to impressions of time and tune? That is to say, teach him the relations and conditions that surround and attend him, as you teach the other the rudiments of music and the key board. Then teach him how to adapt himself to them, as you teach the other the written notes and how to make the tones they represent with the keys. Teach him how to learn the law and keep inside of it, as you teach the other to follow the metronome. Teach him to watch other orderly people, as you teach the other to watch the step of his fellows in the ranks. Then place him in the midst of good influences, as you furnish the other with an instrument with fixed tones and written music, and not expect or require of him that which the natural musician can do. How much farther than this can you go? How much farther than this has any one ever gone in reform?

Sometimes time and tune are latent and dormant, and teaching and example develop them. So, moral sense and perception may be latent and dormant, and teaching and example may make them active. In such case a new and natural mentality will exist that is reformation.

But when you have succeeded with your musician and convict and have created an artificial, mechanical musician of one and an artificial, mechanical moral man of the other, they are helpless unless they can use what they have learned and at the same time make a living. In the tables cited, we find among the ancestry eighty-two per cent. without a means of living other than from hand to mouth. We are left to infer that the convicts were like the ancestry—no table as to accumulations by them being given. Then they have lacked the faculty to acquire and keep the means of living. They must be revolutionized in this respect also. Can that, too, be done mechanically, as the musician is taught to play? Can you find an industrial keyboard with fixed tones, and a metronome to beat time, and written notes that will respond to human effort, and bring forth food and raiment? Yet, without this, there is no practical and permanent reform. Reform does not consist simply in persuading a convict to be moral, but in showing him how to be also practical. A moral man must live. Want, starvation, the sense of an unequal struggle among his fellows, with a sense of injustice, would soon bring demoralization, and he would cease to be a moral man. A man who sits under a tree with some bark around him waiting for birds to bring him something to eat may be a saint—in stories—but he looks through no medium that shows him a view of the moral planes of human thought and action. A man who uses his best energies and faculties to secure bread and shelter, and the home surroundings for which every true human soul longs, and finds his efforts fruitless; while those he can see on all sides enjoy everything he has not, and seemingly without earning or effort, neither has nor can have that vision of moral obligation that will make him struggle hourly to keep his mind on an ideal heaven, a golden rule of justice, and live on a hope of gaining a place in one, and living under the other. The class of people of whom eighty per cent. have " no moral sense "

and "no susceptibility to moral impressions," after reaching
the age of manhood, do not possess any elements that can be
molded into such conditions as will fill their mental field of
view with such a medium as will enable them to see morality
and the things that make up "reformation," as it is understood by reformers and the students and preachers of ethics.

The Bible and Shakspeare are the two greatest teachers the
world has ever known ; and we need not waste time in disput-
ing about the authorship. Men do not begin to fairly comprehend either until they reach fifty years in active and observ-
ant life ; and thence on they grow on one continually. No phase
of life, no condition in the corporal or mental world of being,
nothing that can happen to body or in thought to men, is left
untouched. Every possible relation has received notice and
been touched upon somewhere in each. According to the Bible,
Jehovah tried for centuries to educate and reform a " chosen
people." The result was, dispersion over the face of the earth to
become the foot-balls of all other peoples for centuries more.
If an Infinite Reformer could not succeed, can we finite
reformers do any better or go any farther? He finally abandoned all former methods, reversed the rule of justice, offered
His Son as one great sacrifice in place of all others, and left
the world to take care of itself. When asked to send one
direct from torment to warn those yet living that they might
avoid that "dreadful place," His answer was, "They have
Moses and the prophets. If they will not hear them, neither
would they hear one though he should rise from the dead."
And so man was abandoned of God, with the law for his guide,
and left to learn the great law of compensation and become
subject to it. After eighteen centuries of self-administration,
men are still striving to ignore that law and reach a moral
plane by substituting something else for it ; the most persist-
ent instance of which is evidenced in this "prison question."
We are trying to make reformation of social evils do the work
of prevention. We are trying to make unbridled license of
human impulses produce the virtues of legitimate liberty. We
are trying to maintain social conditions on a foundation of
equal and just rights, while permitting and upholding universal
wrongs. We are trying to reap the harvest of morality and

civil order while sowing the seeds of immorality and disorder.

It is with such an environment that we approach and enter
upon the field of reform in an attempt to make good citizens
out of the criminals that fill the prisons, and seek to fortify
ourselves in the belief that it can be done while we leave open
the increasing sources of supply. Looking through the medium,
not of this environment, but of superstition and an imaginary
hope of the special interposition of the Divine Spirit, we go on
to " save at the spigot and spill at the bunghole," and flatter ourselves that the Reformatory is giving new birth to eighty per
cent. of the mentalities that enter it with eighty per cent. of
their number devoid of moral sense and susceptibility to moral
impressions! I am a pretty strong optimist, but I am not justified in permitting my hopes to hide or ignore truth. I have
not much faith in the prospect or possibility of reforming the
convicts as a body, or any material part of them. I believe
some can be reformed, and many can be partially so, and perhaps a majority may be materially benefitted. Like a temporary relief from pain by use of an opiate, even the worst may
be so improved as to give a temporary lull to the evil impulses
inherent in them, or until stimulated into action by the social
forces that must environ them. But any reformation that is to
be practically beneficial and permanent must begin at the
source instead of at the outlet of the evil. I have already
spoken of that source—the unrestricted sexual license—in the
chapter on Marriage. There, reformation is possible that will
be practically beneficial and permanent. Meantime, reformation at the outlet—the convicts in prison—as far as it is possible, will aid in decreasing the vicious element, and after a few
generations there can be assurance that permanent progress
has been made in actual reform, and the prison question will
no longer be a mystery calling for solution.

There is no doubt about crime having decreased in England
since the present system of treating criminals has been in
operation, and that reformation has been effected to a greater
extent than has ever been accomplished before. But the decrease owes something to the emigration of the criminal elements, to increased opportunities for labor, to a more liberal

legislation for the lower classes, giving them more opportunities for progressive efforts. But, more than all, has been the preventive measures in the supervision and reformation of workhouses and tenements; and the manner of living among the slaves of labor, where they were herded, lived and bred like cattle. The reforms in these respects have been extensive, and the results are visible in the decrease of criminal population.

In this country, while the number of criminals is increasing, something is owing to the importation of many from abroad and the growing evils of crowded centers, producing conditions analogous to those England has been remedying to some extent. Reformation, to a considerable degree, has been effected. The improvement in prisons and in the treatment of prisoners has tended to that result, and will continue to do so. When we shall have secured a system of prisons with chances for classification of persons, labor and teaching, with the abolition of fixed terms and penalties, and the indeterminate sentence alone, with the Bertillon or some other system for identification of prisoners, we may hope for better and more success in reformation of convicts. But we cannot rely on their reformation for any material decrease in their numbers, for reasons already given.

The convict who has never known the elevating influences of a good home, and who has been buffeted by adversity, unable to form associations in which affection or love could find germination and growth, or where there was stimulus to self-respect, personal pride, and ambition to reach and move on a higher level, cannot but be favorably affected on finding that some one is taking an interest in him. When convicted of crime, pronounced by the courts to be a bad man and placed in prison, he feels isolated. He cannot look at himself through the medium that surrounded the court that tried him, as the judge and jury did. He never had lived and moved in any such world of thought, perhaps, as they had inhabited. If he had received religious knowledge and training, he might be susceptible to religious emotions and a personal interest in him would excite such emotional nature as he might have. If he had never received such impressions, another kind of interest would be excited, and for the first time, perhaps, he would see the door opened and gain a glimpse of another world, another kind of life, other motives in life; and a soil might be loosened into which reformatory seed could be cast. Suspicion and distrust might hold him off from response or acceptance a longer or shorter time; but unvarying kindness, and offers of aid and knowledge, guiding him to better thoughts and things for himself, and a view of the real use that can be made and the real aims in the use of the good things within his reach, would sooner or later be favorably responded to; and it scarcely admits of doubt that, there will spring up in the heart of a man who is at all susceptible of emotion, a force that will start in him new lines of thought, and open to his comprehension new views of life. With assurance before him that he can earn a new trial, with help to start in his new efforts, this force will increase in energy, and, aided by the stimulating results of unvarying kindness, teaching, the acquisition of practical knowledge, and a gradual overcoming of the temporary obstructions and difficulties that constantly arise before him, with new perceptions and enlarged vision, reformation will come to a greater or lesser extent. But whether to the extent that will enable him to stand and walk alone when the help is withdrawn, is and must remain unknown until tested by time in each case. There have been no such tests on which answers can be given affirmatively on a majority of cases—for a sufficient length of time to make the answers reliable. To a certain extent affirmative answers can be returned. But the cases tried have not been under the indeterminate sentence. So far, that has not yet obtained generally in legislation, and no true tests can be made until it shall be adopted, in connection with the system for identity, and then, a lapse of sufficient time to test the permanency of the impressions made by the reformatory efforts.

The effort in this work has been, to pass in review existing conditions, with some facts as to the causes of them, and the elements and factors that are inseperable in the subject matter, however we may try to consider it and formulate plans for bettering conditions, and bringing about reformation in both prisons and inmates. The subject is so important, involves so much, in so many directions and relations, and the experience and views of those engaged in various ways in connection with it are so variant, that it is difficult to give such comprehensive views of it as will be generally satisfactory ; and in the order of treatment here assumed more or less repetition is inevitable. But, if we can call attention to only a few truths and practical propositions, the results in combined action with other forces must be ultimately beneficial. We can formulate a general standard of right and wrong that in principle, will be axiomatic, though in practical application it must change in adaptation to changiug social and political conditions. Such a standard I have endeavored to outline in the chapter on legislation. With such a standard, with legislation founded on the princi- ples of justice, with laws relating to prisons, crimes and con- victs, founded on the principle of reformation, and with others tending to the prevention of propagation of degenerate humanity, we shall have reached the limit of human endeavor. I am optimist enough to believe that American intelligence and civilization, under the stimulating influence of liberty, furnishes a soil in which the seed of truth will germinate and fructify if once sown. It may fall mostly by the wayside at first, but some will find fertile spots; and once started, it will in time produce an hundredfold. In this faith I have scat- tered what I believe to be such seed in the contents of this volume, hoping it may prove to be broadcast.

Regarding, as I do, prevention as the most reliable means for beneficial and permanent reform in all things relating to crime, pauperism and the defective classes, as well as in the general elevation of the moral conditions in society and gov- ernment, I hope that, slowly but surely, the knowledge will obtain that marriage is not romance, but the very highest order of business, requiring more deliberation, more care and fore- thought, and entailing more responsibilty than any other act known to humanity. That government will recognize that it has no greater obligation resting on it than to see to it that none have its license to enter into a contract of marriage who are unfit for its relations and duties, as far as human foresight and legal provisions and restraint can prevent. That promiscuous intercourse between the sexes must be prevented by municipal regulations of the social evil, as other evils are regulated under license, and the supervisory charge of a competent board of health, and police enforcement, as I have outlined in the chapter on Marriage. .

Thus would be narrowed the boundaries of the vicious planes on which move the vast hordes of unfortunates calling for state aid and supervision. Thus would come sufficient guarantees for the care, culture and future progress of such dependents as accident and misfortune might thrust into the arms of Charity. Thus would come a solution of the "prison question" in the hope of clearer moral perceptions, more correct views of a true humanity, and greater assurance for the safety and perpetuation of our liberal institutions, under which, morality and dignity should clothe every person who claims that most sovereign of all dignities—the name of AMERICAN CITIZEN.

If, in these pages, I shall have contributed anything that will aid in assuring such a consummation, I shall not have lived in vain.

CHAPTER XV.

EVERYTHING tends to centralization. Vapor in condensing forms globules. Melted lead scattered and falling from a height cools in the same form, and so does water thrown into the air as it separates. Birds gather in flocks, animals in herds, fish in schools, snakes in coils and knots, bees and ants in colonies, monkeys, savages and semi-barbarians in tribes, civilized people in nations, and society into communities and cliques, and they all prey on each other. Power tends in the direction of centralization and usurpation. Weeds grow in clusters and beds and gather in density. Cultivated plants constantly tend to deterioration in spite of every effort. The vegetables and fruits tend to wildness and hybridism and centralization of the characteristics that belong to the indigenous kind from which they originally came and from which they have been changed by cultivation. Humanity is no exception to this rule; and while what we call civilization elevates it far above natural savagery, vice keeps pace with virtue in so-called refinement, and is changed only in the methods of its exhibition. We see occasional instances of what looks like a rose growing out of a dunghill, and they seem like cases of abnormal degeneracy. Is it such? A man or woman of beautiful physical development, of superior intelligence, full of delicate as well as of great accomplishments; the one dressed in the garb of a tramp, leading a tramp's life, and perhaps committing crime. If dressed like a gentleman, he could entertain and edify scholars and statesmen; but his mentality is such that he would pass back to his rags and mingle with tramps beside the strawstack, and listen to obscene recitals while drinking stale beer from an old can and smoking a dirty pipe; the voluntary fellow of vulgar, ignorant, crime-stained vagabonds. The other may be found in the gilded haunts of vice, and also among the dwellers of the slums, the victims of drink and debauchery. There are thousands of these in the garments of women, victims of their own mentalisms and the dominant savagery in men. Can we take them and restore them to a place in the conservatory, as companions of refinement? These are such roses in degenerate soil, gone back to wildness. The attempt to cultivate them in such a soil—which is all we have when once degenerate—is made in the face of history that teaches us the tendency of all things to centralization and retrogression to the original condition from which it has been brought. The rose-bushes separately planted and cultivated constantly tend to wildness—to return to the single-leaf flowers, and finally to the blasted bud with no flower, and only the imperfect bulb from which a bud should but does not come ; and finally, to a centralized patch and then a whole wilderness of briers, unless some stronger growth strangles and crowds them out.

All these, the birds and animals, the fish and bees, the vegetables and fruits and flowers require constant change in treatment, in feeding, in mixing, to produce and preserve for a time only, one variety of superior kind ; and it will not be perpetual, but will deteriorate and be succeeded by a new one, bred from admixture. Next to man the bees and the ants are the most perfect in their intelligence, and they live and plan and act for themselves the most like men, except that they take care to destroy the worthless and save the strongest and most valuable, which man does not ; on the contrary, he strives to make roses out of the fungus of dunghills, knowing that at last it must produce the wilderness of briers.

Man's nature is essentially animal. The barbarian cannot be entirely educated out of him. The dog-feast of the savage, with his clay and ochre paints, his bear's grease and wampum embroidery—the state dinner of the President, with its toothsome roasts and piquant sauces, its silver and flowers and fine raiment, its perfumes and rouge—and the banquet of a king, with its gold and gorgeous trappings, its delicate wines and precedence of place and ceremonies—are one and the same thing, differing only in degree. They are the elements of the barbarian in man which so-called civilization has refined but cannot eradicate, and that crop out in these formalities. On the other hand, no savage was ever naturally a thief. He would be a marauder, a robber, a murderer, but never a petty thief. It remained for civilization—while it made rights of property, law, and courts—to change him into a thief, a forger, an assassin, and many other kinds of a criminal, and teach him how to gild vice and deceive virtue; to check the outflow of his natural impulses to do openly, boldly and above-board, what he now does by secretion, hypocrisy, deceit, lying, and like a coward; for he constantly tends to retrogression and savagery, like the rose to the brier. His vices are refined in one direction and new kinds are bred in another; and the skill given by increase of knowledge is used to make vice successful as well as to give progress to order and morals.

All the barbarities of Indian war and massacre and murder do not exhibit a tithe of the barbarism exhibited in civilized life, in some form, daily. No savage ever rivaled "Jack the Ripper" in unprovoked savagery, or the woman of a great city who lately poured coal oil over her sleeping husband and set him on fire; or the acts of incendiarism, murder and cruelties that crush hearts as well as take life, which we witness around us daily.

It is a serious question whether we have not reached the limits of civilization as an ethical force, and if it will not be succeeded by retrogression and a new and changed one. Has the wave reached the highest impulse, and will it now begin to recede? It began in the east, has crossed two continents, and reached the utmost limit. A new civilization has started along the shores of the Yellow Sea. As the civilization of Egypt, Babylon, Palmyra, On, and the great eastern world, whose mighty ruins surpass our comprehension, and whose literature, so far as deciphered, we must regard as full of scientific and philosophical knowledge, reached a limit, then passed away to be succeeded by that of Greece and Rome and the middle nations, and that in turn by a later in the western nations, which has now reached the Pacific in us, have we not reached the limit of our capacity, and will we not, henceforth, begin to recede, and leave the rhythmic movement to repeat itself as it has done before? We may go on for a time, gaining more knowledge, but will it be used for individual and communal elevation, or for such gratification as must bring on moral deterioration and physical degeneration ?

The facts that come before us with a careful and serious consideration of this prison question are not of a character to encourage us to reject such a possibility. The necessity that compels us to recognize that, amidst all this civilizing force and the enlightenment which attends us, the criminals, the vicious, the demented, deformed and incurably diseased from birth, among rich and poor, the educated and uneducated, as also the hereditary paupers, are increasing in numbers out of all proportion with the general increase of population ; while the vicious and the criminals are becoming more vicious, more reckless, more depraved and barbarous in their methods, and the benefits of education and scientific discovery are used to aid their ingenuity in defying detection and arrest ; with the added facts that, not one in ten of those who commit crime are arrested and convicted by the agents of the law, while the courts of Judge Lynch are held with alarming frequency, and justice is there administered with more certainty than obtains in the courts of law, is one of appaling significance ; and makes it difficult to escape a belief that the seeds of mortality in the civilized nations are germinating and growing, and that, with a rapidity unparalleled in former civilizations, we shall decay as rapidly as we have matured.

In the efforts of reformers to convert the fungi I have referred to into roses for conservatory uses, I am not sanguine of success; I have not confidence in the soil, the strength of the wood fibre, the tenacity of life in the root, or the fragrance or stability of the flowers. The dung-hills are here in great numbers by our own permission and creation, and more are being heaped among us daily, with their fungoid growths, in rapidly increasing patches, fields and wildernesses. Can we change them and their products into rose-beds and keep them so by any means human ingenuity can devise? If we can, we must be able to reverse the operation of natural forces. But we can lessen the hills and their product. We can extirpate the worst, and in some measure change the growth and perfection of some of the fungus into something tolerable in

others existing, here and there, and thus, after some generations, give hope of a renewed chance for the true blessings
that a true civilization would confer.   But will it be attempted?
Not unless a radical change occurs in the public opinion, with
a courage born of intelligent conviction, as to the necessity of
immediate action based on a true comprehension of social and
political ethics.   The man or woman who believes that the
existing soil and growth from whence these classes come can
be tolerated, and that eighty per cent. of the fungi can be converted into useful plants, is a dreamer; with faith in and hope
for the utterly impossible.

In sheer defence we must do something other than we are
doing.   As a contribution to efforts in that direction the
thoughts expressed in this book are presented to such as find
time and disposition to consider them.   They are launched
upon the sea of public opinion with the hope that some of
them will escape shipwreck; will find places where they will
lodge, attract attention, and stimulate serious consideration;
and thus aid a little in support of an energy that can and
should be exerted to better the social conditions, while tending
to the eradication of a false modesty and a better knowledge
of the truth.

www.ingramcontent.com/pod-product-compliance
Lightning Source LLC
Chambersburg PA
CBHW030838270326
41928CB00007B/1113